JANE CHASTAIN

America's First Woman Sportscaster

I'D SPEAK OUT ON THE ISSUES

IF I *only* KNEW^ WHAT TO SAY

Regal BOOKS

A Division of GL Publications
Ventura, California, U.S.A.

Published by Regal Books
A Division of GL Publications
Ventura, California 93006
Printed in U.S.A.

Library of Congress Cataloging-in-Publication Data

Chastain, Jane, 1943-
    I'd speak out on the issues if I only knew what to say.

    Bibliography: p.
    1. Church and the world. 2. Christianity and politics. 3. Christianity and democracy—United States. 4. United States—Politics and government—1981-   . I. Title.
BR115.W6C465   1987   261.1   87-20507
ISBN 0-8307-1185-6

1 2 3 4 5 6 7 8 9 10 / 91 90 89 88 87

Rights for publishing this book in other languages are contracted by Gospel Literature International (GLINT) foundation. GLINT also provides technical help for the adaptation, translation, and publishing of Bible study resources and books in scores of languages worldwide. For further information, contact GLINT, Post Office Box 488, Rosemead, California, 91770, U.S.A., or the publisher.

This book is dedicated
to

Kay Authur, my teacher
Beverly LaHaye, my example

and

Norma DeRossett,

my friend who cared enough to challenge
my walk with the Lord and the depth of my
commitment to the study of His Word.

CONTENTS

FOREWORD

The well-known statement, "ignorance is bliss," is not only deceiving but can produce unpleasant consequences. In fact, bliss from ignorance is only a temporary state of mind. The contentment will cease when reality pulls back the shades of ignorance and reveals the stark truth.

So it is with the facts of our changing society. Many fine people have tried to ignore the philosophy and events that have been undermining our traditional values and morals only to be rudely awakened to the fact that America is in a serious crisis. The very foundation upon which this nation was built is being rewritten, causing the future of our children and the strength of America's families to be threatened.

If America is to survive, we must be armed with information and go to battle daily to protect our freedoms, our children, our heritage and our future. Jane Chastain's book is a reminder that we, as Christians, have not only the right to protect our beliefs, but a responsibility to take a stand for righteousness. This book echoes the teachings of such passages as Hosea 4:6 (NASB), "My people are destroyed for lack of knowledge," and 1 Thessalonians 5:6

(NASB), "So then let us not sleep as others do, but let us be alert and sober," and, along with these important verses, places the practical and effective how-to's of impacting your community and, ultimately, the nation. We must not remain ignorant of the issues. We must avail ourselves of the different sources of material for information and action and be alerted to what is happening and what can be done about it.

We are all called to be politically active, whether the action is simply pulling the handle on election day for candidates who reflect biblical principles, picketing an abortion clinic or running for public office. We all must go to battle for the very soul of our nation, keeping in mind Proverbs 14:34 (NASB) "Righteousness exalts a nation, but sin is a disgrace to any people." The variety of ideas and challenges for action presented within this book are enough to match any reader's ability and schedule.

After reading these pages, no one will be guilty of even thinking, "What can I do? I am only one person." Elections are won or lost by one vote. Bills are passed or defeated and Supreme Court decisions are won or lost by one vote. Elected officials and justices are influenced by one letter (or phone call), plus one letter, plus one letter and so on.

Often just one knowledgeable, brave voice makes a difference. Let that voice be yours. With this book as a foundation, I challenge you to run with endurance the race that is set before you and, as we find in 1 Corinthians 9:24 (NASB), to "run in such a way that you may win."

Beverly LaHaye
President
Concerned Women for America

ACKNOWLEDGMENTS

During the long days and nights I worked preparing this book I was continually uplifted by the prayers and support of faithful friends and the willingness of so many people to share their expertise.

Special thanks to Jo Ellen Allen, Dr. Hani Atrash, David Balsiger, Judie Brown, Ellen Campbell, Scarlett Clark, Dick Digman, Dr. Olga Fairfax, Michael Farris, George Gilder, Jackie Haynes, Michael Jamison, Dr. Arthur Johnson, Elizabeth Kepley, Trudy Koene, Jeanne Lawrence, Barrie Lyons, Connaught Marshner, Coleen McMurray, Earl Mellor, Dr. June O'Neill, George Peate, Jeanne Reed, Carol Polus, Joseph Scheidler, Donald S. Smith, James P. Smith, Michael Schwartz, Sister Paula Vandegaer, Brian Waedman, Dr. and Mrs. Jack Willke, and Connie Youngkin.

I want to acknowledge Helen Sweat and Chuck Benedict for their invaluable help and suggestions, and my editor, Kathi Mills.

And finally, thanks to my wonderful husband and son whose love, encouragement and understanding really made it possible.

INTRODUCTION

It was a big day in my life, near the end of a two week publicity tour for my new syndicated sports show. Tired, but with adrenalin flowing, I was about to address several hundred people as part of the publicity campaign put together by WRC, the NBC-owned station that would carry my program in the nation's capital.

The audience was warm and responsive. I had fun with them and they laughed a lot. Then it happened. As I stepped off the podium, an angry young woman was there to meet me. "I enjoyed your speech," she said abruptly, "but you'd better find a better choice of words."

I had no earthly idea what I could have said to offend her. My TV program was a 90-second vignette, designed to slip neatly into the sports segment of a station's nightly news program where I would come on and explain some aspect of sports. It was fast-paced and humorous. My speech had been more of the same, with some anecdotes about our four months of filming thrown in for good measure. What could I possibly have said to make her so unhappy?

I didn't have to wonder about it for long. She quickly explained that I had used two words that she found objectionable—*ladies* and *gals.*

It's true. I had referred to ladies and gentlemen and gals and guys in my speech. Weren't those terms equal? Should I have said women and gentlemen? Or was she being overly sensitive?

My career began in 1963 at WAGA-TV in Atlanta. That made me the nation's first female sportscaster. I was unaware of that particular honor at the time, and really hadn't noticed all the barriers that had fallen along the way because of it.

I remember the first time I called the Atlanta Braves to set up an interview with a player for my program. The Braves' public relations director had me join him and all the other interviewers (who happened to be male) on the field before the game. He was very nice, deliberately walking me down onto the playing surface. I thought he just wanted to make sure I didn't get lost. How thoughtful!

Upon returning to the station that afternoon, I was surprised to read on the AP and UPI wire services that history had been made—first woman on a National League playing field! I was also surprised that anyone would be interested. And so it was with most of the other barriers. They just fell by the wayside, naturally and without fanfare, as I conducted my work.

Don't let me mislead you; it wasn't all easy. There were those who told me, "It's never been done!" or "A woman can't do that!" But no matter who you are and what you decide you want to do, there always will be people who are ready to tell you the reasons why you shouldn't even try something in the first place.

When I married my husband, Roger, in 1968 and

moved to Raleigh, North Carolina, it was my pleasure to meet the first woman sportswriter. Her name is Mary Garber and she has been working on a newspaper in that state since 1944. While working for WRAL-TV, I quickly learned that you weren't anybody in sports in that area if Mary Garber hadn't written about you. When Mary called for an interview, everyone—from a crusty old coach to the prize college quarterback—said the same thing: "Yes, ma'am!" To Mary and to me, ERA meant only one thing at that time—earned run average.

The following year, Roger and I moved to the Miami area and I went to work for WTVJ-TV, the CBS affiliate. At first, the station would allow me to do only three feature sports stories a week—no hard sports, no anchor position and no live shows. I had to prove myself and that was okay with me. After all, everyone—male or female—must prove themselves when they take a new job. When we left Miami in 1975, my record was ten stories in one day, and I was the sports anchor for the number one news show in town.

But my struggle in Miami to make it to the top was much harder than it should have been. At times I had to fight for my professional life because it was about that time that NOW became more than a three letter word for the present.

When I first arrived in Miami, the public, along with my fellow workers, assumed I was just a *token* woman—a concession to Betty Friedan, Gloria Steinem and company. I resented that. I found it disturbing and degrading, not just for me, but for all women who work hard at what they do, women who don't ask for special privileges but go out and earn them, just like anyone else.

I wasn't one of those women who demanded to be

admitted to a team's dressing room. I simply sent word to the players or coaches that I wanted to do an interview, and they rushed outside, eager to oblige. In some cases, they gave me a better interview than did the other reporters who had to step over each other inside.

In 1977, the National Women's Convention was held in Houston, Texas to celebrate International Women's Year. At that conference, a list of recommendations was drafted and sent to the President of the United States on behalf of the Women of America.

You may remember these proposals: 24-hour-a-day child-care centers; wages for housewives (paid by husbands); abortion on demand; and, their top priority, the endorsement of the ERA—the Equal Rights Amendment.

As the women of NOW went about campaigning for these issues and others, making headlines and nightly newscasts on behalf of the Women of America, I was sure of only one thing—they weren't representing me. I felt left out and frustrated, but what could I do? I was a sportscaster. I didn't know anything about politics and didn't have time to learn. I was not just a working wife any more, I was a working mother, as well. There never seemed to be enough hours in the day.

The turning point for me was 1982. Beverly LaHaye called to ask if I would make some television commercials for an organization she had started in 1978 with five other women in the San Diego area after that National Women's Convention in Houston. These women were as upset over what had been perpetrated in their name as I was, but they decided to do something about it, so they founded Concerned Women of America. I began reading their newsletters. They were short and easy to understand. Slowly, the political maze began to unravel and I became informed, not only on the issues that are important to women today, but also to their families. That's what did it for me. When I realized there were things going on out there in the world that could hurt my family, I decided to *make* the time to get involved.

I soon learned that my enemy was not the National Organization for Women, it is a belief in a value system that "is opposed to all varieties of belief that seek supernatural sanction for their values";[1] a belief that "no deity will save us; we must save ourselves . . . promises of immortal salvation or fear of eternal damnation are illusory and harmful."[2]

Betty Friedan, one of the founders of the women's liberation movement and NOW, and one of the signers of the *Humanist Manifesto II,* stated, "Feminism is an essential stage of humanism. We must keep evolving."[3]

Another prominent feminist leader, Gloria Steinem, shares that philosophy. "By the year 2000 we will, I hope, raise our children to believe in human potential, not God."[4]

The feminist leaders were dedicated to destroying our belief in God and the value system He has given us—my value system, the value system our country was founded upon. No wonder I couldn't go along with it.

I was surprised to find out just how many organizations that are flourishing in this country are built upon this philosophy. I was also surprised to find out how successful they have been in getting this philosophy into our schools, textbooks, courtrooms, radio and TV programs, movies and newspapers in their overall effort to influence and change public opinion.

There is a battle going on and we could lose it. But it's not as one-sided as you might imagine. I have learned that there are a lot of organizations that believe in traditional values. They are out there on the firing lines, too.

I also learned what just one person can do and how one person can really make a difference. I want to share some of that with you.

When I began to understand the issues, I realized that women in this country are being inundated with misinformation—wrong, misleading half-truths. This, of course, is worse than no information at all, because we are being used as pawns by self-interest groups (The National Abortion Federation, for example, represents a 500-million dollar a year male dominated industry) and business enterprises (Virginia Slims Cigarettes-"You've come a long way baby!"), urging us to rally around some issue on behalf of *all womankind* so that they can profit. I was surprised by the number of women who are wise to all of this but have remained silent—not happy, just silent.

I have a special burden in my heart for these women, but men are in this battle also. They, too, are deluged with misinformation. How many times have you heard what a *real* man does or doesn't do?

This book is for all of you who have said to me, to others, or maybe just to yourself, "I'd speak out on the issues if I only knew what to say."

1
DO I DARE GET INVOLVED?

When my son, Blayne, was five, he went home with a friend from Sunday School and came back with his first dirty word. Now it wasn't just any old dirty word, mind you. It was the *primo* dirty word. The kids call it the *F* word.

I did my best to explain why he shouldn't use that word. I exhausted everything available from his limited experience, knowledge and vocabulary. He would listen intently, nod angelically, and when I least expected it, he would use the word again. It was always as if it just slipped out.

I tried explaining again, then demanding, punishing, cajoling, but nothing seemed to work. I guess Blayne knew using that word got my attention like nothing he had ever done before and he just couldn't resist the temptation. I'd had it!

One morning, while jogging with a friend, I related my story, and to my amazement, she asked, "Have you tried washing his mouth out with soap?"

I was appalled! People just didn't do that anymore. It was barbaric! Besides, it might make him sick.

Well, she persuaded me to purchase a bar of Ivory. It's mild, you know. I had it ready in the bathroom and I didn't have to wait very long for the unwelcome word to pop right out again. I picked up my little cherub, marched straight to the bathroom and administered the Ivory. He's 12 now, and to this day I have never heard him utter that word again.

There are a lot more such words. Most of them have four letters. I guess that's why we call them four-letter words.

Vote Is a Four-Letter Word

To many Christians, vote is one of the four-letter words. There are some others that fall into the same category, but don't have four letters—words like politics, caucus, lobbying, Capitol Hill, congressman, and I could go on.

You've heard things like, "Politics is dirty business"; "Politics is corrupt"; "There is no such thing as an honest politician." If those things are true, did you ever stop to wonder how they got that way?

Our First Politicians

Those things certainly weren't true when the foundation of this country was being laid. Before the *Mayflower* landed here, while still at sea, our forefathers drew up a plan that became our first form of government. We know that plan as the Mayflower Compact. It begins, "In the name of God, Amen," and then goes on to say, "Having undertaken [this quest] for the Glory of God and Advancement of the Christian Faith."

Even earlier, in 1606, the Charter for Virginia was drawn up in England: "We, greatly commending and graciously accepting of their desires for the furtherance of so noble a work which may, by the providence of Almighty God, hereafter tend to the glory of His Divine Majesty, in propagating of the Christian religion."

In 1643, the colonies came together for the first time for mutual protection and wrote in the New England Confederation: "Whereas we all came into these parts of America with one and the same end and ayme, namely, to advance the Kingdom of our Lord Jesus Christ, and to enjoy the liberties of the Gospel, in purity with peace." The Confederation also states that, among the several reasons given, the United Colonies formed their "firm and perpetual league" for the purpose of preserving and propagating the truth, and liberties of the Gospel.

Examine the Declaration of Independence: "We hold these Truths to be self-evident, that all Men are created equal, that they are endowed by their Creator with certain unalienable Rights."

James Madison, the principal architect of our Constitution, explained its origin like this: "We have staked the whole of all our political institutions upon the capacity of mankind for self-government, upon the capacity of each and all of us to govern ourselves, to control ourselves, to sustain ourselves according to the Ten Commandments of God."[1]

I think it's safe to say, when we examine the laws that are being enacted today and some that are being interpreted by the courts using the Constitution as a yardstick, that we've come a long way from the goals and objectives of the godly men that were our nation's first politicians.

CAN WE LEGISLATE MORALITY?

There are those among us who say you can't legislate morality. What about immorality? We have already legislated abortion, free sex, no-fault divorce, gambling and pornography. The truth is there is no such thing as a value-free piece of legislation. Every law we have represents someone's set of values. So if you aren't electing lawmakers who believe in your value system, somebody else is electing lawmakers who believe in theirs.

When you get right down to it, there are really only two value systems: one is that of those of us who believe in a Creator God, in whose image we are made; therefore, we, and all others created by Him have intrinsic value. This value system has moral absolutes that are unchangeable, based upon His character and revealed in His word.

The other value system is that of secular humanism, or atheistic humanism: "We reject the divinity of Jesus, the idea that God has intervened miraculously in history or revealed himself . . . men and women are free and are responsible for their own destinies and that they cannot look toward some transcendent Being for salvation";[2] or, if you prefer: Man is the measure of all things—the same man who is a product of matter, energy and chance, so, in this value system, it's easy to see why life (or some life) really isn't worth much. It's the survival of the fittest. There are no absolutes, no right or wrong. Everything is situational. Anything goes.

When you look at it this way, it's easy to see that the people in this country who believe in the latter value system have been working overtime to get laws passed that reflect their views. Ours is a pluralistic democracy. That simply means the people who work the hardest are going to have their views expressed.

The late Christian philosopher Francis Schaeffer said that if you look at a country's laws you will be able to tell what that country's religion is—the laws in India are based on the Hindu religion, the laws in Israel on the Jewish religion, the laws in Russia on atheism, and so on.

What has happened to America? Are we a secular humanist nation? No. According to the latest Gallup poll, 70 percent of our population affirmed the divinity of Jesus Christ and four out of every 10 Americans claimed to be born-again.[3]

What about the Judeo-Christian principles upon which this country was founded? Are they outdated? I think not. When you look at the moral and social decay that abounds, it doesn't take a doctorate in education to realize that our problems were not created by adhering to that value system, but by discarding it. You don't have to be a follower of Christianity or Judaism to recognize that the laws based on the Ten Commandments given to Moses—those same Ten Commandments that James Madison referred to—still work.

What happened to this value system upon which the very foundation of our country was laid? What happened to Christians in government and the Christian influence in this nation's political process?

Why Did Christians Abandon Politics?

It started innocently enough around the beginning of the eighteenth century on a wave of pietism, a religious revival that had already washed over most of Western

Christendom. Pietism began in Germany around 1675 with a man named Philipp Jakob Spener, and arrived here with the second great wave of immigrants, some 200,000 Germans who settled in large numbers in Pennsylvania and northern New York. It took a couple hundred years, but that wave slowly swept across our land, driving Christians out of public arenas nationwide.

All Mr. Spener had really wanted to accomplish was to put a little fire into the formalism that characterized the worship of his day. Spener preached that at the heart of every church there must be a central core of piety. And by "piety" he meant "spirituality," a real and private encounter with the living God—what we now call a "born-again" experience.

You're probably asking yourself about now, "What's wrong with that?" Absolutely nothing. But, in succeeding generations, this private experience that Spener had referred to was taken literally. In an effort to have that private experience, Christians made a run for their prayer closets.

By the nineteenth century, pietism in this country gave way to a first cousin known as individualism. As church leaders began to focus their attention solely on the redemption of the individual, they left the larger concerns to take care of themselves, the theory being that, if the heart of a man could be won, the evils of society would disappear and civil health would be the result. In actuality, Christians began moving out of the streets, out of the schools, out of the media, out of government, out of everything. That left a tremendous vacuum, a vacuum which since has been filled by the secular humanists, the unbelievers and the atheists, who were all only too eager to step in and take over.

Edmund Burke, the great eighteenth-century British statesman, put it best when he said, "All that is necessary for evil to triumph is that good men do nothing."[4]

Have you ever worked hard to perfect a skill, become really good at something and then, for one reason or another, did not use that skill for some time? If you have, then you know how very hard it is to go back to it again. Maybe it's because of a fear that you won't be able to attain the position you once achieved. Well, that's what happened to the Christians in this country as they watched our moral foundations begin to crumble. All that most of them could do was utter, "Somebody better do something!"

Separation of Church and State

Of those who did try to do something, many were scared out. That's right. Those folks with the new power found a few buttons to push that sent Christians running right back to their closets.

One of the most effective of those buttons was, "What about the separation of church and state?" One recent poll showed that, unlike in the past, 25 percent of Americans today actually know that this phrase is not in the Constitution of the United States.[5] Things are looking up! However, this phrase can be found in article 52 of the constitution of the Soviet Union.

Just when did that phrase originate in this country? In 1802, some 15 years after the U.S. Constitution was written, Thomas Jefferson penned it in a letter to the Danbury Baptist Association. At that time, the Baptists in Danbury, Connecticut feared that the Congregationalists would become the preferred denomination. He used that phrase to try to explain to them that the First Amendment guaranteed a state could not establish any one denomination over another. Jefferson said that it placed a wall of separation between the Church and state.

If you examine Jefferson's Second Inaugural Address in 1805, there can be little doubt that he placed that wall of separation around the Church to protect it from the federal government. In the words of President Jefferson: "In matters of religion I have considered that its free exercise is placed by the Constitution independent of the powers of the General Government. I have therefore undertaken on no occasion to prescribe the religious exercises suited to it, but have left them, as the Constitution found them, under the direction and discipline of the church or state authorities acknowledged by the several religious societies."[6]

In 1947, the Supreme Court pulled out that wall of separation phrase from Jefferson's letter to support the *Everson* v. *Board of Education* decision but, since Jefferson is obviously the best interpreter of his own words, it is clear that he felt that wall of separation guarantees us freedom of religion, not freedom *from* religion. And that's just what it says in the wording of the First Amendment: *of* religion!

But don't take Mr. Jefferson's or my word for it. Examine the First Amendment for yourself.

> Congress shall make no law respecting an establishment of religion, or prohibiting the free exercise thereof; or abridging the freedom of speech, or of the press; or the right of the people peaceably to assemble, and to petition the Government for a redress of grievances.

That's all there is. The words *Church* and *state* are not

even mentioned in the First Amendment.

Notice the subject of that extremely long sentence is *Congress*. What does it say about what churches or ministers or Christians can do? Absolutely nothing! It's a one-way street.

Dr. D. James Kennedy made that point while addressing the American Coalition for Traditional Values last year in the nation's capital. Kennedy claims that putting a wall of separation between the Church and state is a distortion of the First Amendment, because a wall inhibits those on both sides equally. That wall would turn it into a two-way street.

To further illustrate, Kennedy took another clause from the First Amendment, the one that says that Congress shall make no law abridging the freedom of the press, and asked, "Can you summarize that part by saying there should be a wall of separation between the press and the state? Certainly not, because that would mean the state could say nothing about the press and the press could say nothing about the state."[7] Doesn't sound like our Constitution, does it?

In fact, the Bill of Rights—the first 10 amendments to the Constitution—was a result of some hard work by clergymen and others who felt the Constitution as originally written gave the government too much power. Throughout history, people have been persecuted for their religious beliefs. The desire for religious freedom was one of the major reasons that led to the settlement of this country. Our forefathers suffered hardships, many fought and died, for the freedom that so often is taken casually today.

When you become a Christian, you do not give up your citizenship, not at all. As Christians we not only have a right to get involved in politics, we have a responsibility.

There are biblical mandates for doing so. Exodus 18:21 is one:

> But select capable men from all the people—men who fear God, trustworthy men who hate dishonest gain—and appoint them as officials over thousands, hundreds, fifties and tens.

See also Job 34:17; Proverbs 11:11,14; 12:24.

It's Hard to Get Back

Psalm 125:3 tells us, "The scepter of the wicked will not remain over the land allotted to the righteous." Today, many Christians are unaware and some simply don't care that the scepter has passed from the righteous into the hands of the wicked. It's hard to reverse years of chronic inactivity.

George Barna and William Paul McKay put today's Christians under a microscope, using the latest research and national survey information. In their book *Vital Signs*, they offered this observation: "By and large Christians are politically illiterate. Despite heightened awareness in some issue areas, the majority of Christians remain inactive and unconcerned about policy developments."[8]

Barna and McKay address some of the problems caused by this chronic inactivity (p. 28). They point out that less than 20 percent of this nation's Christians claim to participate frequently in political activities, and only about 4 percent have ever run for public office.

But there are other reasons we fail to get involved, and some are to our credit. According to Barna and McKay, Christians are more satisfied with the nature and the quality of their lives than their non-Christian counterparts. They go on to say that 64 percent of Christians were found to be very happy with their community, as compared to only 55 percent of non-Christians. They also found that 82 percent of the born-again public say they often feel happy about their life, compared to 67 percent of non-Christians. When you are happy and satisfied, you have less motivation to spend some of your precious free time on political activities. But you must—we must!

Could it be that many Christians have been so busy enjoying the good life that they haven't even noticed a battle is being waged for control of their land and that they are about to lose? If you read the papers or hear the news on radio and TV, you are well aware of the battle, and it may seem just a little overwhelming. I pulled the following excerpts from the first three pages of the newspaper I read this morning:

> As of mid-July, the Centers for Disease Control in Atlanta reported 22,319 full-blown AIDS cases in adults nationwide, 316 in children under 13.[9]

> Under the law (Ca)—and under penalty of a $10,000 fine and jail time—an AIDS blood test cannot be given without the written, informed consent of the subject . . . . There have been abused children, (and) you have to ask permission of the suspected abuser if you can test him (the abuser), and by law he can refuse.[10]

> (Barry) Lynn (ACLU legislative director) expressed the belief that there will be less

enforcement of obscenity laws nationwide, despite the federal pornography commission's call for a sweeping crackdown. "Frankly, I think that most law enforcement people don't see pornography as dangerous."[11]

See what I mean? It would be so easy just to close this book right now and play follow-the-leader back into the prayer closet.

When we pray the Lord's Prayer we say, "Thy will be done on earth as it is in heaven." What does that mean? I believe it means that we are to "occupy until he comes" (see Luke 19:13, *KJV*). God works through us. No, He certainly doesn't have to or need to. He does it out of love. He allows us, as His children to do His work here on earth.

I am reminded of the first few times my son wanted to help me make breakfast. The result? The kitchen full of dirty dishes, pancake batter running down the stove and the omelet on the floor. It would have been so much easier, and quicker, if he hadn't helped.

It is awesome when you think about God allowing us to help. How can we refuse His offer? How can we turn away His love? We must go to our prayer closets but, when we pray, we must do more than ask for forgiveness and give God our wish lists; we must ask for His guidance.

What I tell you in the dark, speak in the daylight; what is whispered in your ear, proclaim from the roofs (Matt. 10:27).

We are called to be lights in the world, not just lights in the churches. If you are afraid, tell God.

For God has not given us a spirit of fear, but of power and of love and of a sound mind (2 Tim. 1:7, NKJV).

Confess that fear and ask God to take it away, to heal you of that fear. Our heavenly father is so faithful.

The Sovereign Lord is my strength (Hab. 3:19).

The Bible not only gives us mandates for Christian citizenship, it's full of promises for those who seek to live out their faith as well:

If my people, who are called by my name, will humble themselves and pray and seek my face and turn from their wicked ways, then will I hear from heaven and will forgive their sin and will heal their land (2 Chron. 7:14).

See also Psalm 34:15,17.

After we pray and after we ask God's guidance, if we are to live out our faith, we have to roll up our sleeves and be willing to go to work.

Do not be overcome by evil, but overcome evil with good (Rom. 12:21).

When God gives us a command He also gives us the power to obey, but this does not belittle the command nor lessen the responsibility. Stuart Briscoe explains this so eloquently in his study on the book of Philippians, *Bound for Joy.* "God takes His own Word so seriously that He makes the power available for it to be obeyed. And it intensifies the responsibility because no one can evade the command of God with any kind of excuse if God's answer to the excuse is, 'I gave you the command and I gave you the power; there is nothing else to say.'"[12]

When we go to the Word, there can be little doubt about what we are to do. Martin Luther left us this timeless message:

> If I profess with the loudest voice and clearest exposition every portion of the truth of God except precisely that little point in which the world and the devil are at the moment attacking, I am not confessing Christ, however boldly I may be professing Christ. Where the battle rages, there the loyalty of the soldier is proved and to be steady on all the battlefield is mere flight and disgrace if he flinches at that one point.[13]

Will "vote," "politics," "caucus," "lobbying," "Capitol Hill" and "congressman" still be dirty words when my child and others of his generation are grown? It depends on you and me. Are you willing to roll up your sleeves and get to work?

Blessed is the nation whose God is the Lord
(Ps. 33:12).

2
How Do I Get Started?

I have no way of knowing where you are right now when it comes to understanding the issues and being able to share information about them with others, but believe me when I tell you this—you're further along than I was when I began to look for answers. I can promise you that. On a scale from 1 to 10, I was a 0.

My career had become all consuming. When I wasn't actually working, I went to ball games, or listened to them on the radio, or watched them on television just to keep up. I always carried the daily newspapers' sport sections and several sports magazines with me wherever I went just in case I had a few spare moments. At night I cut out my *paper dolls* (stories on athletes), as Roger called them, to file away.

I was accustomed to having to prove myself, and I took pride in being one of the most knowledgeable sportscasters around, but when it came to any other subject, forget it. When someone mentioned a well known political figure or movie star, my favorite retort was, "What team does he play for?"

Even after I began to study the issues that were important to me, I found I had trouble articulating my views. One day, while talking with a female broadcaster friend of mine, the Equal Rights Amendment came up. Don't ask me how it entered our conversation but, when I suddenly realized we were on opposite ends of that issue, I found I couldn't put the words together to explain my position.

Then she said, "Well, all it says is that equality of rights under the law shall not be denied or abridged by the United States or by any state on account of sex. What could be wrong with that?"

She had me. I realized I didn't even know the wording of the ERA. Was that really it? Was that all? I had been reading reports on why it was a bad piece of legislation and I had bought that view, sight unseen, without really studying the issue myself. Was it really that bad? I wasn't sure my position was tenable.

"I'll have to check my files for the information," I stammered. "I'll call you back."

Be Prepared

Has that ever happened to you? I can still remember how embarrassed I was. I did go to the files I had created for the material I was going to really study someday when I had the time. Do you have those kinds of files yet? Well, I did study the material that very day, and then I sent it to my friend. I didn't call her back as I had promised, though, because I still didn't trust myself in a discussion.

I learned something from that conversation. I learned not to let issues like that sneak up on me. In fact, I became rather adept at avoiding them altogether. But it wasn't easy. They seemed to pop up everywhere.

Underneath I felt guilty because, by being silent, I found myself often condoning issues that I knew were wrong. Has that ever happened to you?

I also felt guilty because I knew I could make a difference if only . . . if only what? "I get emotional over these issues. That's it. They are just too important to me," I would tell myself. "That's why I can't articulate them."

Deep down inside, I think I knew the answer all along. I could make a difference—if—I would put as much importance on the things that mattered to me personally as I did on the things that mattered to me professionally. If I would carefully analyze and weigh the facts surrounding the issues the way I did teams, batting averages and passing percentages, I would know what to say to explain my view. The emotion was often a result of frustration over my inability to articulate the facts.

Nothing but the Facts

When you get right down to it, there are only two basic kinds of information—fact and opinion. A fact is a statement about reality. It deals with something that exists or has existed. Facts can be proven or verified. They are indisputable, incontestable and, here's the best part, noncontroversial.

Opinion, on the other hand, is someone's beliefs or feelings on a subject. As a sportscaster, I had to earn the right to give an opinion. We call it editorial commentary, and that right came only after years of broadcasting facts and nothing but the facts.

I'm not suggesting that you never offer an opinion. Opinions based on careful study and observation can be very valuable. We call it reasoning. Expert opinion is often introduced by lawyers as evidence in trials. Just be aware of the difference between fact and opinion. Feelings often tarnish the facts and cause people to question your information. They can turn good solid truths into mere speculation.

What I am suggesting is that you arm yourself with the facts and see just how far they will take you. I think you'll be surprised that, when presented with factual information, most intelligent human beings will make the right choice—naturally. They don't have to be prodded, cajoled, badgered or coaxed into it.

I know just what you're thinking right now. "All this sounds like a lot of work. I'd really like to, but I just don't have the time." No one does, so break it down into small parts. Begin this very moment by looking under the table of contents of this book for the issues chapters and select the one that means the most to you right now. Then make a commitment to yourself to become articulate on that one issue. After you've chosen an issue, come back and finish this chapter before moving ahead with your issue.

Now, stop and congratulate yourself. You have just taken the first step in becoming an informed, articulate, responsible American citizen. Recognize that the first step is the hardest. It'll be downhill from now on. I promise.

Next, if you're shy, buy yourself one of those pretty bookcovers or use a plain brown wrapper and cover this book. It may sound crazy, but you can take it with you to do your homework wherever you go—whenever you find yourself waiting in line, at the doctor, the haircutter, the car wash, etc. The cover will help you avoid any premature discussions before you're ready, discussions that might cause you to lose your confidence. If you're not shy, just tell anyone who asks that you're studying the issues that are important to every American so you can discuss them later. Then suggest that, for now, they buy their own copy.

When you begin reading the issue chapters (not just yet) you will find a short introduction to each issue, followed by questions and answers. These questions and answers are designed to get you through everything from a conversation with your next door neighbor to an interview on national TV. There is no way to anticipate all that might be asked or the actual form the questions will take, but if you will study these, put them in your own words and commit them to memory, you'll be armed with the facts and material you need to educate others when the opportunity presents itself. When we "Put on the full armor of God" (see Eph. 6:11), the opportunity will present itself. One thing I've learned is that God doesn't waste anything.

The questions numbered 1,2,3, etc., are the ones that are sure to come up when one of these issues is discussed. The questions labeled a,b,c, etc., are your back-up material.

Set Your Goals

Now, let's get back to that word *educate*. That is your goal. You can't really change someone's mind or force them to think the way you do. You wouldn't want to do that, even if you could. But, by presenting clear, concise, factual information to others, they may change their own minds or decide it's time to stand up and be counted on an issue they've never taken the time to consider before. That is your goal.

You've made a commitment. You've selected your issue and you're ready to get started. But before you do, create a timetable for yourself and set some realistic goals. *Don't* skip this part. This is absolutely necessary if you are really serious about following through.

As you read the section on the first issue you have selected, assess your ability to memorize. This comes easily for some folks, but it's extremely difficult for others. Then decide how many questions you are going to commit to memory each day. It may be only one, and that's okay. Just *own* that question at the end of the day. Be able to answer it anyway it comes to you: backward, forward, sideways or upside down. Begin each day that follows with a quick review, and you will own them for life.

Now, add up the days it will take you to master the issue. Count them off on your calendar and circle the date on which you will have achieved your goal. When you get there, celebrate and go on to issue number two. (If there's a particular issue you're interested in that's not included in the issues chapters, use those chapters as a guide to develop a set of questions and answers for that issue.)

As you progress, new information and facts surrounding one of your issues may come to light and you will want to add these to your repertoire. Try making up your own questions and answers. Just keep them clear and concise. Stick to straightforward, simple, unemotional questions and statements and you'll do fine.

Oh, I almost forgot. As you work on the issues chapters, keep reading the rest of this book. By the time you've finished, you'll be making a difference.

3
WHAT IS COMPARABLE WORTH?

Feminist leaders say comparable worth is, "The issue of the decade and beyond."[1] Wrapped in the cloak of *fairness and equality,* comparable worth (CW) is the greatest threat to our free market system this nation has ever known. It's a sock in the chops of the free enterprise system that has provided more opportunity for more people than any other in the history of the world.

Like the Equal Rights Amendment, comparable worth began with such momentum that many people feel it's a train that cannot be stopped. But the education process has begun on this issue, and you and your friends must be a part of it if this highly explosive freight car is to be derailed.

Its proponents say it is designed to bring blue-collar income to pink-collar workers, more specifically—to eliminate the difference in the average wages paid women and the average wages paid men. You're probably well aware that there is a difference, but it's not as great as most of us have been led to believe.

MISLEADING STATISTICS

"Fifty-nine cents" became the battle cry of certain feminist groups after Geraldine Ferraro delivered her vice-presidential nomination acceptance speech at the Democratic Convention in 1984 in San Francisco. Fifty-nine cents is what Ms. Ferraro said women earned compared to men in the *same* job.[2] Linda Chavez, who was the staff director of the U.S. Commission on Civil Rights, said that Ms. Ferraro was either *misinformed* or *misspoke*.[3] To discuss comparable worth, we need to know what the difference between men's and women's pay is and why it exists.

In actuality, women make 65 cents for every dollar a man earns, bases on annual income,[4] or 75 cents if you base it hourly for doing *different* jobs. The 1983 figure that Ms. Ferraro could have used was 64 cents, based on annual earnings,[5] or 72 cents, based on hourly earnings.[6] If you break the hourly figures down further, women between the ages of 20-24 earn 92 cents for every dollar a man earns in that age bracket; 25- to 35-year-old women earn 84 cents; but for women of all ages who have never married, compared to men in the same category, the difference is only five cents—they earn 95 cents, compared to a dollar for men. The difference is greatest, almost 29 cents, between men who are married and living with their spouses and women who are married, living with their spouses.[7]

Is this discrimination? The feminists say it is, and they want this disparity eliminated through comparable worth.

HOW WOULD THIS BE ACCOMPLISHED?

Instead of supply and demand determining wages for various positions, which is what we have now, comparable worth advocates would create a panel or board to set wages, using an elaborate point system based on the principle that all jobs have certain levels of knowledge, experience, education, effort and responsibility. If these CW advocates have their way, this panel would tell not only the government, but eventually all private business what can be paid their employees. This would be the law of the land. Now, this panel or board wouldn't set wages all by itself. It would be aided by consulting firms who spend years and cubic dollars comparing dissimilar jobs.

Consider the fact that the Census Bureau now lists some 23,000 job titles in its index. Can you imagine the size of the bureaucracy necessary to compare the worth of 23,000 jobs, or the legal chaos that would follow?

The best definition I've found for comparable worth so far is "equal pay for unequal work." Is this whole thing beginning to sound a little loony to you? Well, you're in good company. The chairman of the Civil Rights Commission, Clarence Pendleton, Jr., agrees with you. He went as far as to say that it is "the looniest idea since Looney Tunes came on the scene."[8]

But hang in here with me because, loony or not, Congress is examining the issues, and 23 states already have completed comparable worth job evaluation studies. Based on these studies, lawsuits have been filed and millions of taxpayers' dollars have been spent.[9]

The movement began in Washington state in 1974 when then governor Dan Evans was persuaded to study the difference in earnings between men and women. The subjective point system worked out by Norman D. Willis & Associates rated a food service worker equal to a truck driver, a mail carrier equal to a clerk typist, a gardener equal to a librarian, and a police officer equal to a short-hand secretary. In all cases, the lower paying job was held by a woman.[10] A lawsuit by the American Federation of State, County, and Municipal Employees Union followed, claiming sex discrimination, which resulted in a $482 million-settlement.[11]

ULTIMATELY, WOMEN WILL LOSE

Does all this sound like a great deal for women trapped in the lower paying jobs? It certainly is for many of those women now affected by the strikes, suits and legislation, but opponents of comparable worth feel that all of us ultimately will lose if CW continues unchecked.

University of Washington economics lecturer Paul Heyne says the real problem starts when comparable worth is applied to the private sector. "If they try to force employers to pay more—employers who don't have tax-payers to fund them—the employers are going to find ways to get along with fewer of that kind of employee. They're going to substitute machinery and reorganize procedures."[12]

The number of jobs available to women will further be reduced as men begin moving into these traditional women's areas because apprenticeship, physical risk and unpleasant working conditions in many of their jobs have virtually been ignored in CW plans produced to date. Also, many women who have taken nontraditional jobs to reap the financial rewards will likely reevaluate their decisions, eliminating the progress made thus far in job integration.

This is not wild speculation. Australia passed a form of comparable worth for both the public and private sector in 1972. Within five years, female unemployment rose, the number of women working part-time increased, and the growth of female participation in the labor force slowed. [13]

The U.S. Commission on Civil Rights conducted exhaustive hearings in the spring and summer of 1984. In 1985, it concluded that "sex-based wage discrimination is a serious matter. However, there are currently existing ways to remedy it, and the implementation of the unsound and misplaced concept of comparable worth would be a serious error." In discussing the *wage gap* the Commission concluded it results for the most part "from a variety of things having nothing to do with discrimination by employers."[14]

The Commission's recommendations were as follows:

> 1. We recommend that the Federal civil rights enforcement agencies, including the Equal Employment Opportunity Commission, reject comparable worth and rely instead on the principle of equal pay for equal work. Moreover, we recommend that the Justice Department resist comparable worth doctrine in appropriate litigation and advance the policies outlined in recommendations 11 through 17 (contained in report) in cases involving pay for different jobs.
> 2. We recommend that Congress not adopt legislation that would establish comparable worth doctrine in the setting of wages in the Federal or private sector.

You don't hear or read much about this report when comparable worth legislation is proposed or when the subject is discussed. CW proponents are not going to bring it up. That's our job—yours and mine. The report is a matter of public record. The proceedings and recommendations are in a three-volume set in most public libraries. It's available from the Commission if you'll write to them. Just address your letter to the United States Commission on Civil Rights, Washington, D.C. 20425.

CW proponents seem to believe there is some male conspiracy to keep women in lower paying jobs. What they tend to forget is that many women have different needs, particularly women with children. There are many factors to consider in choosing a job besides wage: regular hours, pleasant surroundings, location, easy entry and exit, etc. They also refuse to acknowledge the following facts: the average woman works only 70 percent as long for a given employer;[15] the average women works only 35 hours a week, compared to 42 for the average man.[16]

George Gilder, the author of *Wealth and Poverty* and *Men and Marriage,* points out that women prefer to work part-time, and that a woman is 11 times more likely to leave her job than a man. Gilder says even female physicians earn less money than their male counterparts because they take 38 percent fewer patients an hour and choose to work fewer hours.

FREEDOM TO MAKE CHOICES

Choose—I think that's the key word. Here in the United States we still have the freedom to choose our profession. You don't have that freedom in every country. If we don't like the wage we are being paid as a laundry worker, we can take a job as a garbage collector, a fire fighter, or a mail carrier. And when we, as women, take one of those jobs, we are guaranteed by law (see chapter 5 on ERA) that we will receive the same pay as men, with the same seniority, for doing the same work.

Comparable worth advocates seek to make everyone equal. That's the basic principle of socialism. The question we must ask is, equal to what? In most forms of socialism, equal tends to mean equal to the lowest common denominator. When comparable worth is discussed, you don't find people lining up to take a salary cut to achieve this goal.

A democracy does not guarantee that everyone will be equal. It guarantees that everyone will have an equal opportunity. There is a difference.

IMPORTANT NOTE. Before you begin any discussion on comparable worth, you must know the real figures on what women make, compared to men. The hourly figures in this section are based on third quarter 1986 numbers. Be as up to date as possible.

Call or write periodically to the Bureau of Labor Statistics, Department of Labor, 200 Constitution Ave., N.W. Washington, D.C. 20210, (202) 523-1371. Tell them you want to compare women's wages to men's, using both an annual and an hourly figure. The department will have the annual figure readily available, but they will have to give you the latest average weekly earnings of full-time workers, along with the corresponding hours worked per week, and you will have to figure the hourly earnings. Then, using the hourly figures, find what percent the women's hours are, compared to men's. If it is 75 percent of the men's figure, than a woman makes 75 cents for every dollar made by a man. If you're not a whiz at math, get a friend to do it for you.

Be specific about the information you want from the Department of Labor. Don't be shy about asking for this information. Remember, the Bureau of Labor Statistics is there to help us, and we pay for the operation of this department through our taxes.

If you are in an interview situation, some figure will very likely be given in the introduction to the discussion. If this figure is incorrect, or if it is an annual figure, simply ignore the first question and say, "Before I answer that question, I would like to question the figure you gave" or, "Before I answer that question, I would like to bring everyone up to date on the difference in earnings for men and women." Then give the correct figure. You cannot begin a discussion based on incorrect or outdated information.

The second thing you need to know is that the terms *comparable worth* and *pay equity* are identical. Pay equity is a recent adaptation to make comparable worth more palatable. You must remember that, in defining an issue, it is a tremendous advantage to come up with a term or group of words that, taken at face value, produce no objections. On the surface, pay equity sounds wonderful. Who could possibly object to that? It was the same with the Equal Rights Amendment.

Your next job in any discussion is to rebuke the term *pay equity*. You'll see some examples in the questions that follow.

QUESTIONS AND ANSWERS

1. *What is pay equity?*

Pay equity is a recent term applied to a system of wage-setting known as *comparable worth*, in an effort to dress it up and make it more palatable.

2. *What is comparable worth?*

Comparable worth is government intervention into the wage-setting process of our free market system. Under comparable worth, instead of pay being based on an agreement between the employee—in many cases a union—and employer, pay (or worth) is established by an evaluator using an elaborate point system. The evaluator rates each job and then tells the employer what the wages will be for that job.

3. *What's wrong with that?*

It's surrendering our economic freedoms to the government. It's unfair to almost everyone and it destroys incentive.

4. *I understand that it's giving the government more power, but why is it unfair and how will it destroy incentive?*

Suppose I have the same job as the guy who sits next to me, but I work twice as hard. My employer will be unable to give me a raise or pay me more because our wages are set by the government.

5. *Isn't pay equity just another way of saying equal pay for equal work.*

No. Comparable worth (I don't like the term *pay equity* because it is misleading) is *equal pay for unequal work.*

6. *What do you mean?*

The aim of comparable worth proponents is to eliminate the difference in the average wage paid women and the average wage paid men. Since men and women continue to work, for the most part, in different occupations, the only way to accomplish this is to compare dissimilar jobs.

7. *Comparable worth proponents say it's equal pay for equally valuable jobs, that certain jobs are actually similar when studied in terms of the skill, effort and responsibility they require. What's wrong with doing that?*

Today the average man makes more than the average woman for a variety of reasons, so the evaluation system you begin with can't be neutral and bring about the desired result; and, if the evaluation system you begin with isn't neutral, it's unfair.

8. *A lot of people would say that what's unfair is the system that created this disparity in the first place. How do you answer that?*

It's not the system that created the disparity, but the fact that most married women who enter the work force enter with different priorities than do married men. These women deliberately choose occupations where entry and exit are easy; the average woman in her prime earning years is 11 times more likely to leave the work force voluntarily, and she works only 70 percent as long for a given employer as a man does.[17] The average woman in the work force works only 35.2 hours a week, compared to 41.8 for a man;[18] even female physicians earn less money than their male counterparts because they see 38 percent fewer patients per hour and work fewer hours. Conversely, single women who work full time for a long period of time have earned about as much as their single male peers.[19]

9. *Formal job evaluation is more than 100 years old. It became widespread during World War II and is used today by both government and private employers, so why not have everyone operate under this practice?*

Very few businesses use job evaluations, and those that do use *benchmark* jobs to adjust wages to prevailing market rates. That's not comparable worth.

10. *Some states like Minnesota are using comparable worth pay scales now. You must admit, it's working at the state level.*

It's working in that the state has conducted a study, rated its jobs and is paying people accordingly. It is costing Minnesota approximately 4 percent of its yearly payroll. That was $22 million in the first year alone. Additionally, Minnesota couldn't get enough doctors to work in state hospitals with the salary set by the evaluator, so they are already making exceptions. [20]

11. *Isn't it worth 4 percent to correct this disparity?*

This has created a disparity in the amount of money all Minnesota taxpayers are able to bring home to their families now, and when you look at the cost, should comparable worth be carried over to the private sector, the dollars are astounding. The National Chamber of Commerce did a study in 1984 and estimated the cost in the first year to be between $300 billion to $400 billion which now must be adjusted for inflation. That $300 billion to $400 billion would be paid by all of us as consumers.

12. *Wouldn't those additional dollars paid by taxpayers and consumers mean more money in the pockets of working women?*

Initially, yes, at least for those women in jobs directly affected by the suits and legislation; however, in the end, there will be less opportunities and fewer jobs for women. We will all lose if we destroy the free enterprise system that has provided more opportunity for more people than any other system in the world.

13. *Can you prove that?*

Our overall standard of living is one of the world's best. As to the effects on opportunity for women, we need to look at what happened in Australia. That country adopted a form of comparable worth in the public and private sectors. After five years, female unemployment rose, the growth of female participation in the labor force slowed and the number of women working part–time increased.[21]

14. *Is it fair that a woman with an M.A. in English literature, working as a secretary, makes less than a truck driver with a high school education who delivers canned goods?*

Many other facts besides education determine wages in our free market system, such as physical demands, regular hours, length of day, working conditions and physical risk, to name just a few. Besides, in our country, if a woman doesn't like what she is making as a secretary, she can quit and become a truck driver.

15. *How do you explain the fact that so many women with college educations are trapped in low-paying jobs?*

I strongly question whether all these women you referred to are actually trapped. One must remember that all college graduates don't get good jobs. A recent report by the Association of American Colleges shows that many college students simply do not use their freedom of choice to select courses that give them a good education and prepare them for the real world.[22]

16. *How do you explain the fact that the average college educated male makes more than a female with the same amount of education?*

If you'll check employment trends in a study such as the Northwestern Endicott Report, you will see that college majors in most demand are electrical engineering and computer science. Next in line are mechanical engineering, accounting and mathematics. The higher paying majors are still graduating a higher number of men, and the lower paying majors, a higher number of women. The number of women entering these fields is rising, but the function of our government is to protect our freedom to choose, not to protect us from our choices.

17. *A recent study showed that female and male M.B.A. graduates of Columbia University started out making the same salaries in 1970, but within 10 years the women were earning only four-fifths of the men's salaries. Is this discrimination?*

You must consider the choices made by each woman after leaving Columbia. One important consideration is, did she marry and have children? The wage disparity is greatest between women who are married and living with their spouses than any other group because they tend to try to balance their careers with family responsibilities. They may be willing to take less money to get other benefits. Conversely, when you compare the wages of women who have never been married to men in the same category, using an hourly figure, women make 95 cents to every dollar made by men.[23]

17-A. *Should these differences in any category you mention, whether great or small, be acceptable?*

The difference in wages for men and women who have never been married is hardly calculable; however, differences can be found in comparing almost any group. For instance, Japanese Americans earn more than Americans of European descent; Catholics earn more than Protestants; West Indian blacks earn more on the average than American-born blacks. As to the married women, would you question their ability to make rational decisions about their needs and desires? That's called freedom.

18. *Do you recognize that any form of discrimination exists in the job market?*

Yes, discrimination does exist and we should do everything possible to eliminate it. Equal pay for equal work has been the law of the land since the 1963 Equal Pay Act and was reinforced by Title VII of the Civil Rights Act in 1964. Further, women are guaranteed equal opportunity in employment by the Equal Employment Opportunity Act of 1972.

One of the biggest problems is education. There are

cases where men and women do exactly the same thing and the employer will give them different titles to try to get around the law, but in most cases, women don't even know they are being discriminated against. We all like to feel as if we are exempt from the unpleasant aspects of life. More often than not, a woman who is being discriminated against simply doesn't know what the fellow in the next office is earning.

19. *Doesn't Title VII of the Civil Rights Act, which makes it unlawful for employers to segregate or classify employees in any way that would adversely affect them because of sex or other specified reasons, support comparable worth claims?*

A case involving a comparable worth claim, *County of Washington* v. *Gunther,* went all the way to the Supreme Court in 1981. Although the high court ruled in favor of the plaintiff, it took great care to state that the concept of comparable worth was not the basis for its ruling.[24] Lower courts have been divided on this issue; however, Title VII nowhere indicates that an employer's reliance on market factors, resulting in different wages for different jobs, is illegal, regardless of whether a subjective analysis suggests that the jobs are comparable.[25]

20. *What should a woman do to avoid being discriminated against?*

Be aware, ask questions, get the facts. If you suspect that you are a victim of discrimination, find out if there are other considerations. How long has the guy in the next office been on the job, how much experience or training did he bring with him, how much does he actually produce?

Then compare that to your own productivity. If you are in sales, for instance, and his sales are 25 percent higher than yours, increase your productivity before you ask for a raise.

21. *What if you find a real case of discrimination?*

I believe in going to your employer first with the right spirit. Maybe he really isn't aware that he is discriminating and will correct it. If your productivity is up, he won't want to lose you, and he knows you can change jobs. Men, as well as women, are often paid less than they are worth because they are willing to settle for that; they don't ask for more. Or they are unwilling to change jobs, which allows an unscrupulous employer to take advantage of them.

22. *Can you find outside help?*

Certainly. Contact your local Equal Employment Opportunity Commission office. Also, private attorneys love cases like this, because it's an automatic win if there is discrimination. But don't get bogged down on this and let it keep you from advancing in another job with another employer. It's counterproductive.

23. *What if you are in a field or job where the pay is low overall? Comparable worth proponents say certain jobs have more intrinsic value than other jobs and should be paid accordingly.*

Why do diamonds cost more than water? Water certainly is more essential. Chocolates cost more than soybeans and soybeans clearly have more nutritional value. Price is obviously determined by many things other than intrinsic worth.

24. *But is this fair when we are dealing with people, not products?*

In those comparable worth studies, in Minnesota, a registered nurse, a chemist and a social worker all have equal worth. However, in Iowa, the nurse is worth 29 percent more than the social worker, who in turn is worth 11 percent more than the chemist. In Vermont, the social worker is worth 10 percent more than the nurse, who in turn is worth 10 percent more than the chemist. [26] There is no system of complete fairness. In communist and socialist countries, where they try to make everyone equal, we need to ask ourselves, equal to what? Equal generally means the lowest common denominator. It's the government that ends up with the big bucks. A democracy does not guarantee that everyone will be equal; it guarantees that everyone will have an equal opportunity. There is a difference.

25. *Don't you at least agree that comparable worth studies could be worthwhile and should be implemented?*

Absolutely not! When a study is done, like the one in Washington state, politicians are often motivated to confess they were guilty of discrimination because it's in their political best interest to do so. And why not? They don't have to pay the bill. The taxpayers pay the bill. It is not easy to stand up to the lobbying by special interest groups. If you can get government officials to confess to discrimination, then the study finds there is discrimination. When a court case follows, which is what usually happens, the judge has no choice but to rule that there was discrimination, based on the evidence in the study.

26. *But there are comparable worth plans in effect that rate jobs on the basis of intrinsic value, which many people believe to be fairer than the marketplace, which adjusts itself to the forces of supply and demand.*

The people who like the plans now in existence are those who have folks with their own biases on the evaluation team. Most of these plans judge worth by paper credentials instead of by apprenticeship and experience, and by ignoring physical risk, danger and unpleasant working conditions. The Willis plan in Washington state, for example, awards less than 5 percent of the possible points to physical demands and working environment combined. The National Academy of Sciences study of 1981 says "There are no definite tests of the fairness of the choice of compensable factors" and goes on to say "The process is inherently judgmental."[27] The U.S. Commission on Civil Rights also did a study in 1984 and concluded that the theory of comparable worth "is profoundly and irretrievably flawed."[28]

27. *If important bodies such as the Civil Rights Commission have given these opinions, why are so many states doing studies and working out comparable worth plans?*

It's a perfect example of the power of special interest groups. Politicians lack guts. They're calling it *pay equity* now. It's cloaked in the mantle of fairness and the general public is still poorly educated on the issue.

28. *What would you suggest we might do to close the wage gap?*

First, we must recognize that implementing comparable worth in the '80s to solve the economic problems of women would be like raising the pay of redcaps (porters, bellhops) in the '50s to solve the economic problems of black Americans. We must put the emphasis where it truly belongs—on education and opportunity.

29. *Where should we begin?*

By encouraging our daughters to fully assess their goals in employment and earnings as well as their abilities *before* entering college or any other form of higher education. We must also encourage women in the work force to be informed on the laws that now exist to ensure fair treatment and equal opportunity in the marketplace, and we must work to see that these are vigorously enforced. But, above all, we must dispel the myth that worth is measured solely by dollars. We must recognize that laundry workers, nurses, computer scientists and bank presidents all have the same worth in the sight of God, and that money, alone, would be a poor reason for choosing a career.

4

IS ABORTION ALWAYS WRONG?

This is a subject that, by now, has affected you in a very personal way. If it hasn't, it very likely will in the not too distant future.

Since the Supreme Court made abortion on demand the law of the land in its landmark *Roe* v. *Wade* decision back in 1973, over 18 million legal abortions have been performed here in the United States, over 1.5 million a year, 4,100 a day, 171 an hour, or about 3 abortions every minute.

ABORTION IS PERSONAL

Approximately five people are directly involved in every abortion decision, which means 90 million people may have already participated in a legal decision to end the life of a developing child in the womb. That's over half the adult population in this country—maybe even half the people in your very own family!

Would you know if members of your family had been involved in abortion? Within your immediate family, I hope so; but today, so many mothers and fathers, sisters and brothers don't know until they are called in when it's too late, in an emergency. With very few exceptions, abortion is a subject nobody wants to think about, much less discuss, especially those 90 million who have already been involved. I know. I'm one of them.

Several years ago, one of my closest friends—I'll call her Anna—phoned me and told me matter-of-factly that she was pregnant and had decided to have an abortion. It took me totally by surprise. Anna had always wanted a baby of her own and had even talked about trying to adopt as a single parent.

"Why not have this baby?" I suggested.

Anna explained that the father was a married man and of another race. It would ruin her career. She had already made the arrangements and asked me to take her to the hospital and cover for her. I did. After all, it was her decision, her choice and it was perfectly legal.

We didn't discuss it in the car that day as I drove her to a hospital just outside of Los Angeles, but while I sat by her bed as the time approached for her "operation," Anna told me that she could see the heartbeat and tried to show me.

"That's nonsense!" I said. "It's just a glob of tissue." She wanted to talk, but I wouldn't let her.

I told myself I was right. I had to be right. They wouldn't have done it if it were anything more.

When Anna was returned to the room several hours later and tucked into her bed, she wanted to talk again. "Look," she said pulling up her hospital gown, "the heartbeat is gone."

I didn't look, and I wouldn't let her discuss it anymore. I thanked God it wasn't me lying there and put it out of my mind, or at least as far back into the catacombs of my mind as it would go.

Abortion—the word came up again and again as the controversy over its legality grew, and every time it did, I thanked God I never had to make a decision for myself on whether it was right or wrong—or make a *choice,* as it is called.

In 1981, I was approached to introduce a film for television on abortion called *A Matter of Choice.* It was based on the docudrama "Assignment Life."

"I don't think so," I stammered in response. "You see, I've never really thought much about abortion."

The production company asked me to look at the rough cut anyway and sent it over that afternoon.

I watched the film and I learned a lot. I learned that by the time a woman knows she's pregnant, at six weeks, just two weeks after she's missed her first menstrual period, the developing child is quite recognizably human, the heart is beating and there are brain waves. By two months, just after a woman has missed her second period, the embryonic period is over; the baby is moving about in the amniotic fluid and the brain is complete. Lungs and heart are almost fully developed, taste buds and olfactory apparatus (sense of smell) are present. Its stomach secretes gastric juices. Ovaries and testes are descending and fingers and toes are distinct. The baby is able to respond to touch and tickling and has a recognizably baby-like face. Two months—a woman can seldom confirm a pregnancy and make arrangements to terminate it before that.

I realized then that my friend had been right. The heart of her developing baby was beating at that time (what we saw was probably from her own aorta).

I must have watched that footage four times that day. I

didn't want to say yes to the production company. Abortion was just too controversial. Psychologist James Dobson was one of many who participated in that film and his words stayed with me. He said that if we as Christians stood by and didn't do anything, we were as guilty as the abortionist wielding the knife. We would be held accountable by God.

I watched the film one more time that day, this time with my husband, Roger. When it was over he turned to me and said, "There is only one decision you can make. You've got to do it!" Roger was right.

ABORTION IS DANGEROUS

I learned a lot of other things from that film. I learned about the physical damage and medical complications of those *safe, legal* abortions, not just to the pregnant woman, but to a wanted child later on. A woman who has had an abortion in her first pregnancy has twice the chance of a miscarriage later on and twice the chance of having a stillbirth. She is three times more likely to have a baby born prematurely, and she is more likely to have trouble in labor. Her chance of an ectopic pregnancy (where the baby nests in the tube because of scar tissue) are 400 to 800 percent greater, and 5 to 10 percent of all women who have abortions find they have aborted the only child they will ever conceive.

Once again I sat at my friend Anna's bedside the day her uterus was removed. She was childless.

In 1984, I was asked to host a film on abortion called *Conceived in Liberty*. In that film I had a chance to interview some of the most influential people involved in that issue in our nation today. It was while doing that film that I really became aware of the tremendous amount of unresolved psychological problems left in abortion's wake. I discovered a number of organizations that had sprung up nationwide for victims of abortion, which now minister to others who are still hurting. These organizations also spend much of their time trying to prevent others from having abortions.

But it was hard for me to believe this problem was as serious or as widespread as some believed it to be. I remember one particular interview with attorney Gloria Allred, who told me that she once had an illegal abortion and was dedicated to insuring this right for all women. She didn't look like she was hurting.

Conceived in Liberty was released just before Concerned Women for America's first national convention in Washington, D.C., and was shown on the evening of September 14, 1984 to approximately 2,000 women. The staff was not prepared for the reaction to the film. Shortly after it began, woman after woman drifted into the lobby in tears, discovering hurts that had been buried for years.

My thoughts went to Anna. Was she hurting too? The pro-choice people I had interviewed in that film had referred to the guilt as a *religious problem.* Anna did not believe in God, and had steadfastly refused to go to church or listen to the message of the gospel. I had prayed for her for years. She was extremely self-reliant, but I had refused to let her talk about the abortion then, and neither of us had brought it up again. I was sure she had put this behind her, but I had to know.

The next time we were together I said, "Anna, you know I love you and I've always tried to do the best for you as your friend, but there was one time I failed you, and I need to talk about it." I said the word *abortion* and she burst into tears. She too had been hurting all those years.

WE MUST TALK ABOUT IT

That's my story and the story of my friend. We're just two of those 90 million people who already have been touched by this plague that has divided our nation and cheapened our society. The other 89,999,998 folks don't want to think about it or talk about it either, but we must—they must.

With over half of our adult population already having been personally involved in an abortion decision, discussing this issue is unlike any of the others. Many of these people are still hurting; many are hurting and don't even know why, or they know and have not yet admitted it to themselves.

When you discuss abortion you have to assume you are striking a nerve and you must be prepared to help with the hurts that remain, or at least be able to acknowledge them with love, and refer these people to someone who can help. You'll find some suggestions in the appendices of this book under "Resource Organizations."

Christians can be forgiven by the blood of Jesus. When you are discussing this issue with other Christians, you can begin with that message of hope. But can we, as Christians, go on with our lives and do nothing more? The Bible is very clear about this. We cannot! Exodus 20:13 (RSV) states, "You shall not kill," Proverbs 24:11,12 says, "Rescue those being led away to death; hold back those staggering toward slaughter. If you say, 'but we knew nothing about this,' does not he who weighs the heart perceive it?" See also Proverbs 21:13 and Matthew 25:45.

Let me quickly point out here that when you are discussing this issue (or any other) you should not use Scripture with those who do not believe the Bible is the inspired Word of God. If they do not believe in God, then the Bible is just a lot of mumbo jumbo and, not only are you wasting your time, you may come across as *holier-than-thou* or be regarded as a *religious crazy.*

SCIENCE AND THE BIBLE AGREE

Regardless of their religious persuasion (or lack of it), most people agree that it's wrong to kill another human being; but, is the developing child in the womb a human being? Here is one point where medical science and the Bible are in complete accord.

A recent Senate subcommittee report stated, "Physicians, biologists, and other scientists agree that conception marks the beginning of the life of a human being—a being that is alive and is a member of the human species. There is overwhelming agreement on this point in countless medical, biological, and scientific writings."[1]

An article in *Newsweek* said that, "In most serious debates, however, it is taken as a biological fact that a fetus is alive, human and unique."[2]

> Before I formed you in the womb I knew you,
> before you were born I set you apart (Jer. 1:5)

> As you do not know how the spirit comes to the bones in the womb of a woman with child, so you do not know the work of God who makes everything (Eccles. 11:5, RSV).

If medicine, biology, science and religion are in one

accord, why is abortion on demand law in this country? It is ironic that in 1973, while *Roe* v. *Wade* and its companion case, *Doe* v. *Bolton,* were being decided, an amazing new technology known as *realtime ultrasound imaging* had just begun being used, which provided fetologists a window to the womb. In 1976, the first scientific papers based on that technology appeared. Justice Sandra Day O'Connor wrote in a June, 1983 dissent that, "The Roe framework is clearly on a collision course with itself."[3]

The ultrasound technology caused Dr. Bernard Nathanson, who ran the largest abortion clinic in the western world and was a founding member of the National Abortion Rights Action League, to change his mind and defect to the pro-life movement in 1975. In the film *Conceived in Liberty,* Dr. Nathanson told me that the Supreme Court decision that legalized abortion was "made in a scientific vacuum. Based on any of the data we had at that time, it was probably at least a logical decision, but certainly a decision born strictly out of ignorance."[4]

Nathanson is far from alone. Less than three percent of his medical colleagues, or 8,700 of over 300,000 physicians in the United States, will provide abortions to their patients[5] and many of the ones who do have adopted cutoff dates of 10 to 12 weeks into the pregnancy.[6]

But what about that 3 percent who still do abortions? According to Nathanson, "The overriding factor here is money. The abortion industry is a half-billion-dollar-a-year industry (in this country). One is always reluctant to assassinate Santa Claus."[7]

UNINFORMED CHOICES

Anna's words to me keep ringing in my ear: "If we

knew then what we know now, I wouldn't have done it, and you wouldn't have let me."

Why didn't we know? But even more relevant, with all the scientific developments in the past decade, are most women who are faced with the abortion choice today told about the health risk and potential dangers before they decide? Are they informed on the status of the tiny life within their womb? In most cases, they are not.

Why? Because most are in a state of panic upon receiving the unwelcome news of an unplanned pregnancy, and often are rushed into a decision on abortion. The Supreme Court ruled a state-imposed 24-hour waiting period unconstitutional in 1983. Also, a pregnant teenager can be removed from school and given an abortion without her parents' knowledge or consent.

The counseling at an abortion clinic usually consists of focusing on the pregnant woman's fears, and getting rid of them. "Women are made to feel it's best they do not know (about the procedure) and those who are embarrassed to bring up their fears are not encouraged to do so."[8]

Counseling at school is usually from material provided by Planned Parenthood. With over 53 abortion facilities nationwide, Planned Parenthood is the largest provider of abortions in America today. In both cases, it's like letting the fox into the chicken coop.

Should informed consent be necessary as it is with any other surgical procedure? On June 11, 1986, the Supreme Court said *no* in *Thornburgh* v. *American College of Obstetricians and Gynecologists*. In deciding this case, the high court struck down a Pennsylvania regulation that had required physicians to tell the woman about the particular medical risk of the abortion procedure versus those of carrying the baby to term, and to offer her information describing the anatomical and physiological characteristics of her unborn child. [9] The state had also required information be given about agencies available to help these women if they decided instead to give birth. [10]

WHERE DO WE STAND?

Are we in too deep? Have we gone too far to stop the killing? By the grace of God, we have not! The *Thornburgh* v. *American College* decision was by a slim 5-4 ruling, as compared to 7-2 for *Roe* v. *Wade* in 1973. In dissent, Justice Byron White concluded that the division on the court is "symptomatic" of its "own insecurity over its handiwork in *Roe* v. *Wade* and the cases following that decision."[11] He called that 1973 decision "fundamentally misguided" and urged that it be overruled. [12]

But what about us, the people of America? Where do we stand? A poll produced by the Gallup organization for *Newsweek Magazine* in 1985 showed that 38 percent of us are now questioning our position on the subject and only 21 percent of us feel that abortion should be legal in all circumstances.[13] I wonder how many of those polled know that's exactly what we have now—unlimited, unrestricted abortion at any time up until the actual moment of birth.

Before you can discuss abortion you must be completely familiar with that 1973 *Roe* v. *Wade* decision by the Supreme Court, with all its implications.

The ruling divided pregnancy into three different stages:

0-3 months: No restrictions, anything goes.

3-6 months: From three months to viability.

6-9 months: The states can ban the abortion of a viable fetus unless the mother's life or health is affected. Health is further defined as psychological, emotional, physical or familial. Since three of these four categories are subjective, in effect, if a woman can find a physician willing to perform an abortion, she has a constitutional right to obtain one in America at any time through the nine months of pregnancy, right up to birth.[14]

These late-term abortions are commonly of three types: saline amniocentesis, Prostaglandin and hysterotomy. In the first procedure, a salt solution is injected into the baby's amniotic sac by inserting a large needle through the wall of the woman's abdomen. The baby, after breathing and swallowing the salt solution, dies. Then the mother goes into labor, often a day later, and delivers a dead baby. It usually takes over an hour to kill the baby this way. You can just imagine what is going through the mind of the mother as her baby struggles and convulses inside her body.

The Prostaglandin abortion involves a drug made from the human hormone prostaglandin, manufactured by the Upjohn Company primarily for this purpose. It can be given to the mother in a variety of ways and causes violent labor and delivery. The baby occasionally survives this extremely rough trip down the birth canal. One of the major complications of this type of abortion is a live birth. Again, you can imagine the effect on the unsuspecting mother. The Center for Disease Control in Atlanta estimates that 400 to 500 abortion-live births occur every

year in this country, so it's basically an everyday occur-
rence.[15] Although approved by the Food and Drug Administration, Prostaglandin abortions have a complication rate
of 42.6 percent.[16]

The hysterotomy is just an early Caesarian section
(where the mother's abdomen is cut open). If the physician
is to protect himself legally, he must reach into the uterus
and clamp off the cord or cut it so that the baby is smoth-
ered to death before being removed. If he lifts the baby
out still breathing, a child has technically been born and
should be accorded the rights of any other citizen of this
country. About 13,000 viable babies are killed—after the
mother's twenty-first week of pregnancy—every year in
this country by one of these three methods.[17]

And what about the women involved? What a choice
they had—the agony of saline or Prostaglandin, or having
their abdomens sliced open in a hysterotomy! Given the
real facts beforehand and the choice once again, I wonder
how many of them would have waited a couple of months,
weeks, or maybe even days for a natural and safer birth. I
wonder just how many of those women faced with a late
pregnancy, or any pregnancy, who say, "I just couldn't
have the baby and give it up for adoption," really know
what the other choice involves. It's no wonder so many
claim there are really *two* victims in every abortion.

"Abortion is a social problem and must be solved by
humane social solutions, not surgical holocaust." That
statement was made by Dr. Bernard Nathanson, a secular
humanist.[18]

Can we, as Christians, take any other position?

> I know your works, that you are neither cold
> nor hot. I could wish you were cold nor hot. So

then because you are lukewarm, and neither hot or cold, I will spew you out of My mouth (Rev. 3:15-16, NKJ).

TELL IT LIKE IT IS!

It is important to remember that, when you are discussing or debating this issue with a knowledgeable pro-abortion person, he or she will attempt to throw you off by turning it into a discussion of women's rights in general or the social issues of the day. You must not let this happen. While filming *Conceived in Liberty,* I learned that the pro-abortion organizations actually hold training sessions for members of Congress who support their views. They train them on how to avoid discussing what an abortion is, and how to turn it into a *nonissue.*

Another tactic of the abortion industry is to paint anyone who is pro-life as uncaring. They try to give a picture of the woman, faced with an unwanted pregnancy, as alone against the world. Be prepared to take every opportunity to mention all the groups available for help. Have local groups and phone numbers available at all times and give them whenever you speak. Someone's life depends on it! Also mention the organizations set up specifically for victims of abortion as often as you can. It's hard for pro-choice people to paint abortions as safe when there are large groups of women who have had abortions that are organized and anxious to proclaim they are not safe.

Also avoid the vocabulary of the abortion industry. They have desensitizing words for almost everything, terms such as *fetal tissue* or *a product of conception.* Although *fetus* is a proper term for a developing human from three months after conception to birth, pro-lifers prefer using *baby* or *unborn child*. Abortion is not simply *having your period restored* or *termination of pregnancy*—it is *killing a baby*.

Don't dignify the process. Those places that are set up solely for the purpose of doing abortions are not *clinics*. Clinics are for healing people. Abortion mills are little more than processing centers, staffed by abortionists and operated with all the impersonal, mechanical regularity of an assembly line. Learn to recognize the vocabulary of the abortion industry and replace it with your own. Tell it like it is!

Finally, get the four *myths* in right at the beginning. Practice converting any first question that's thrown at you to that answer. Question one is an example. It's the best way I know to get your listener's attention.

QUESTIONS AND ANSWERS

1. *You are opposed to abortion, as many others are in this country today, but do you think you should be allowed to take away someone else's right to choose?*

I think we all have the right to be informed before we choose. I believe that women have been given more misinformation in the area of abortion than in any other. Let me point out that what we have created in this country is a half-billion-dollar-a-year industry! One-and-a-half million women in this country choose abortion every year based on four myths perpetrated by this industry. *Number one:* that unborn babies aren't babies, but globs of tissue. *Number two:* that having an abortion is as safe as having a tooth pulled. *Number three:* that it won't affect their childbearing chances later on. And *number four:* that nobody gets hurt.

2. *Isn't telling a woman that it's a baby and not a collection of cells or a glob of tissue in the early stages of pregnancy, when most abortions occur, just as misleading?*

The important thing for women to understand is that by the time they know they are pregnant, just after they have skipped their first menstrual period at about six weeks, brain waves are detectable and the heart is beating. Between the sixth and seventh week, the nerves connecting the spinal cord are in place. And, by the end of the eighth week, a miniature infant is clearly formed, all body systems are present, and from that time on, the changes in the body will be primarily in dimension and refinement of working parts. Do you think that most women would go through with an abortion if they knew they weren't just choosing to get rid of a glob of tissue that someday, somehow, would develop into a baby?

3. *The law says that women have the right to choose.*

The law you refer to came in the form of the Supreme Court decision in 1973 known as *Roe* v. *Wade* and the companion case *Doe* v. *Bolton.* Since that time, the law and medical science have been, in the words of Justice Sandra Day O'Connor, "on a collision course."[19] The Roe decision was reached before the first studies were released using the technology of realtime ultrasound imaging, which now gives us the ability to watch the developing child in the womb. Since that time, fetologists and embryologists have been successfully treating the developing child in *utero* (in the womb). Dr. Bernard Nathanson, who at one time ran the largest abortion clinic in the world and helped found the National Abortion Rights Action League, changed his mind after ultrasound. He says that the Supreme Court decision was made in a "scientific vacuum" and based on "a world-is-flat theory," and that the law must be changed. [20]

4. *The American College of Obstetricians and Gynecologists has taken a pro-choice stand and, obviously, there are many doctors who do abortions and feel they are doing the right thing. What about those doctors?*

I question whether they really feel they are doing the right thing. To use the words of Doctor Nathanson again, "One is always reluctant to assassinate Santa Claus." [21] Doctors who do abortions are part of the group that has the most to gain financially. Again, we're talking about a half-billion dollar a year industry. [22] But obstetricians and gynecologists, even within that organization, are divided on the abortion issue. Only about 3 percent of all physicians in this country are willing to provide abortions. [23] There is another organization, called the American Association of Pro-Life Obstetricians and Gynecologists, who feel that abortion is wrong.

5. *Dr. Nathanson has become somewhat famous for a documentary using a realtime ultrasound videotape of a 12-week suction abortion, The Silent Scream. Haven't many experts attacked its authenticity?*

What's an expert? And who is a neutral expert? Certainly not someone from Planned Parenthood, the largest provider of abortions in America, or someone from the National Abortion Rights Action League. None of the objections to this monumental work came from people who were bona fide experts in ultrasound or fetology. The producer of the film was so conscientious, he published a book that contains not only the text of the documentary, but a well-documented paper refuting all charges. If anyone is interested, it's available from American Portrait Films in Anaheim, California or from pro-life organizations.

6. *Wasn't the main criticism that the brain of the fetus was not developed enough to respond to pain?*

That specific objection was that the *cortex* of the fetus was not sufficiently developed at 12 weeks. The cortex, which is fully developed later on in pregnancy, only allows the unborn baby to evaluate the sensation of pain, in addition to being able to feel and react to it. [24] A fully developed cortex is not absolutely necessary for normal human activity. [25] In fact, all the body parts needed to experience pain are well developed in the 12-week-old unborn baby. [26]

7. *What are those body parts?*

The nerves, spinal cord and the thalamus of the brain, where sensations like heat, cold, pain and touch first become conscious. [27]

8. *Wasn't President Reagan the first to bring up the issue of fetal pain?*

You might say he focused the nation's attention on that issue in an effort to point out the inhumanity of abortion at a speech delivered to the National Religious Broadcasters in 1984. In that speech, he said that fetuses often suffer "long and agonizing" pain during abortion. [28]

9. Wasn't that charge refuted by some important physicians?

Yes, by Dr. Ervin Nichols of the American College of Obstetricians and Gynecologists (ACOG). However, a group of 26 prominent professors, including pain specialists and two past presidents of ACOG got together, wrote a letter and held a news conference to say the president was on "firmly established ground."[29]

10. *But Dr. Nichols said he was unaware of any evidence that pain is perceived by a fetus, but that they may have "demonstrated neurological reflexes."*[30]

That is what he said. Another doctor, Dominick Purpura, the current dean at Albert Einstein School of Medicine, in trying to discredit *The Silent Scream,* brought up the cortex argument and said the fetus didn't have the awareness for *personhood* at 12 weeks. Purpura put that boundary at seven months.[31] I find that a little odd since I'm sure he, and every doctor in the world, must be aware of cases in which babies have been born at 20 and 21 weeks—that's four-and-a-half months—and have developed normally. Everyone can see that those children born at four-and-a-half to five months respond to pain.

11. *Dr. Nathanson's new film, Eclipse of Reason, shows an abortion on a four-and-a-half month old fetus (through the use of fiber-optics inside the womb, with a camera positioned at the mother's feet.) How do you feel about this film.*

I think it's very hard to dispute what an abortion is after seeing it.

12. *In that film, Nathanson focuses on the number of late-term abortions. He claims 8 percent are done in the second and third trimester. Hasn't that figure been disputed?*

That's about all that could be disputed about that film, but if you will check the conservative figures released by the Centers for Disease Control in Atlanta for the last four available years (1980-1983), about 10 percent of abortions are performed after 13 weeks, which would be 130,000 each year.[32]

13. *What is the stand of American Medical Association (AMA) on abortion?*

The AMA policy maintains that if killing of the unborn is legal, then it is also ethical.[33] But, interestingly enough, only 42 percent of our nation's doctors pay dues to the AMA.[34]

14. *What is the youngest known baby to have survived?*

The youngest baby that I know about is Marcus Richardson. He was born at 19 weeks, 6 days on New Year's Day in 1972, at University Hospital in Cincinnati, and is a perfectly normal child. And in study after study of these tiny preemies that make it, a very small percentage have any significant problems.

15. *Would lowering the age of viability solve the major objections of the people who are unhappy with Roe v. Wade.*

No, because viability is really not a factor in *Roe* v. *Wade*. After viability, the ruling allows the states to ban the abortion of a viable baby unless the mother's physical or mental well-being is affected. It's the mental part that makes this completely unenforceable, since it's impossible for anyone to determine a mother's mental well-being except the mother herself. There are no real restrictions! In fact, 13,000 babies—conservative figure—are killed after the mother's 21st week of pregnancy every year.[35]

16. *Wouldn't some of these babies have been born with a handicap?*

If Helen Keller had been conceived in our day, there is a chance she would never have been born, and society would have been the loser. There are many well-documented studies that show the frustrations of handicapped children appear to be no greater than that of non-handicapped children.[36] The Surgeon General of the United States, Dr. C. Everett Koop, who has spent most of his life working with children born with abnormalities and defects, says he never has had an old patient come back and ask him why he worked so hard to save his life, or a parent who said, "Why did you work so hard to save my child?"[37] In fact, there has never been a single organization of parents of mentally retarded children that has ever endorsed abortion.[38] Selective killing of the unborn has already led to selective killing of those already born.

17. *In what way?*

In June of 1986, the Supreme Court struck down the *Baby Doe* regulations. In a 5-3 decision, the justices ruled that the Department of Health and Human Services had no authority to pressure hospitals to treat handicapped newborns without parental consent.

(If you are discussing this question with someone who believes in God and in the Bible, you can reinforce your answer with Scripture.) That the Lord makes and uses the imperfect is evidenced in such verses as the following:

> The Lord said to him, "Who gave man his mouth? Who makes him deaf or mute? Who gives him sight or makes him blind? Is it not I, the Lord" (Exod. 4:11).

> Woe to him who quarrels with his Maker, to him who is but a potsherd among the potsherds on the ground. Does the clay say to the potter, "What are you making?" Does your work say, "He has no hands"? Woe to him who says to his father, "What have you begotten?" or to his mother, "What have you brought to birth?" This is what the Lord says—the Holy One of Israel, and its Maker: Concerning things to come, do you question me about my children, or give me orders about the work of my hands? (Isa. 45:9-11).

18. *But is it fair to force a handicapped or retarded child on a family that doesn't want it?*

There are people on waiting lists to adopt these children. Call the Spina Bifida Association of America, the National Down's Syndrome Society, your local Crisis Pregnancy Center or one of the pro-life organizations for information.

19. *What about abortion in the case of rape?*

Rape that results in pregnancy is extremely rare. There

have been studies on rape victims that have been treated at hospitals immediately after the rape with drugs that have been 100 percent effective in preventing pregnancy. [39] Studies in Pennsylvania and Minnesota show that as many as 5,000 rapes have occurred without a single pregnancy. [40] But if pregnancy does occur, the woman needs extraordinary care. Destroying a child conceived through rape does not end the trauma; it will not blot out the memory of the assault. We should not add the guilt of killing her unborn child to all her other problems. Abortion is the same kind of violence as was the rape.

20. *What about incest?*

This is a crime where the victim is usually very young. It's a quiet crime, and the girl often is far along before anyone finds out. Abortions on young victims of incest are extremely hazardous; the younger the mother, the more likely she will suffer sterility. [41] And with a very advanced pregnancy, the problem is compounded with a viable, unborn child.

21. *Why are abortions more dangerous for young girls?*

Because the opening in the cervix is much smaller in a young girl. These muscles are often stretched open by the abortionist in about one minute, while the birth process would take many hours. In many cases, these muscles are damaged beyond repair. The young girl will not be aware of this until much later when she conceives and tries to carry a child to term. A cervix often will not support a baby when the muscles have been stretched or torn. [42]

Studies in Canada indicate that the complication rate is as high as 30 percent among teenagers aged 15 to 17 who have had abortions[43] and yet, in most states, a young girl can be given an abortion without her parents' knowledge or permission. There is no required waiting period, and abortionists no longer have to inform women about the dangers or the status of the pregnancy (Supreme Court ruling, June, 1986). Young girls, more often than not, are rushed into a procedure that could affect them for the rest of their lives.

21-A. *You mentioned that the cervix is opened rather quickly during an abortion. What about the use of laminaria?*

Laminaria is a small piece of dehydrated seaweed, which is placed in the cervix and left there overnight.[44] It reduces the risk of damage to the cervix, but doesn't eliminate it completely.[45] Laminaria is rarely used in abortions, because it requires two visits and cuts into profits. There are very few regulations imposed on the abortion facilities. The abortionist rarely sees the woman again, so most won't go to the trouble of using laminaria.

22. *Earlier, you referred to what you called the myth that an abortion is as safe as having a tooth pulled. I've heard that; where did it come from?*

From Alan Guttmacher, the former president of Planned Parenthood. That statement was included in a pamphlet, "Abortion, A Woman's Guide," in 1965. Guttmacher said abortion was "as safe as having a wisdom tooth pulled." Later, the phrase was reprinted by abortionists, leaving out the word *wisdom.*[46]

The Center for Disease Control reports that 11 women died in 1982 from legal abortions in this country.[47]

Many more deaths occur due to complications that arise later, but the cause is listed as something other than abortion, such as blood poisoning. Also, many physicians who ultimately treat these women are reluctant to name abortion as the cause of death because they don't want to embarrass the woman's family.

Thousands more are maimed in abortion mills all over the country. Many of them advertise, "We can do it cheaper." Then, they run women through and, in most cases, never see them again. Organizations for abortion victims, such as American Victims of Abortion, Open Arms, and Women Exploited by Abortion will tell you that there is no such thing as safe, legal abortion.

23. *What about the 5,000 to 10,000 women a year who died from illegal abortions before the Roe v. Wade decision in 1973?*

Those figures were the ones given out by abortion proponents, and they are grossly inflated, totally false. The Center for Disease Control (CDC) reported that 39 women died as a result of illegal abortions in 1972, the year before *Roe* v. *Wade*.[48] Dr. Nathanson confessed that he and the rest of the people at N.A.R.A.L. (formerly National Association for the Repeal of Abortion Laws; now National Abortion Rights Action League) used these false figures in his book *Aborting America*.[49] It's a tragedy when any woman dies from an abortion, legal or illegal. It's also a tragedy in this country that women are led to believe by those who are making a profit that abortion is the big cure-all; and that they are not told beforehand that, if they have an abortion, they have almost twice the chance of a miscarriage later on, twice the chance of having a baby born dead, three times the chance that they will have a baby born prematurely and three times the chance that they will have trouble in labor.[50] Their chances for an ectopic, or tubal, pregnancy are also dramatically increased.[51] When the Supreme Court says doctors do not have to inform patients of the dangers of abortion as they do with any other surgery, you must ask yourself, "Are women really better off today?"

24. *Surely you don't think that all deaths due to illegal abortions were reported?*

No, no more than I believe that all deaths due to legal abortions are reported, nor that all the complications from abortions are reported. Officials at the Center for Disease Control in Atlanta readily admit this. All information on abortion is sketchy. Information that could be of tremendous help to women in terms of their health is not required to be given by those performing abortions. When the Supreme Court struck down a Pennsylvania law that had required the abortionists to inform women on the dangers of the abortion procedure, the court also struck down a regulation that required physicians to file certain data about abortions and their patients for public use. This regulation did not require the name of the patient be recorded, only the health information. Justice Sandra Day O'Connor said that this decision makes it "painfully clear that no legal rule or doctrine is safe from ad hoc nullification by this court when an occasion for its application arises in a case involving state regulation of abortion."[52]

25. *What about the woman's right to privacy?*

If the doctor isn't required to put a name with a report,

that's certainly private enough. It is clear that the court does not have the best interest of the women of this country at heart. Justice White said that decision, which struck down the so-called *informed consent* regulations, was "symptomatic of the Court's own insecurity over its handiwork in *Roe* v. *Wade*."[53]

As far as the right to privacy, which the court pulled out of the hat in deciding *Roe* v. *Wade,* the court manufactured that right in 1965 in deciding another case. It is not in the Constitution. The court balked in 1986 at recognizing a privacy right for homosexual sodomy. The privacy doctrine is tenuous at best. Does a right to privacy prevail when you see or hear someone abusing a child at home?

26. *All right, you feel that abortion is wrong, so it's wrong for you, but why not leave it at that and let others choose for themselves?*

If tomorrow our lawmakers decide it is legal to kill 10-year-old children, would you say, "It's wrong for me, but I'll let other people decide for themselves"? I hope not!

27. *But we're not talking about 10-year-old children; we're talking about fetuses.*

Fetus is a Latin word that means "unborn baby." And that's what doctors, who are concerned with saving lives, usually call the child in the womb. What is the difference between a baby the day before it's born and the day after? There is no difference. It's wrong to take the life of another innocent human being.

28. *Isn't it just as wrong to impose your moral beliefs on someone else?*

We do that all the time in the form of laws. In effect, we impose our belief on a person who would like to kill another human being who happens to be living outside the womb.

29. *Well, is an unborn baby a human being?*

It's not a flower or a tree or an earthworm. It's human and it's alive and, on that point, science, medicine and biology all agree.

30. *But there are those who do not agree, who say there must be a certain level of consciousness, a certain degree of viability or physical development before one is a human being. What about their views?*

That's a philosophical argument, not a biological one. Some of those people also believe a certain degree of mental or physical perfection should be reached; many want a waiting period established after birth to make sure the child does not have a disease or an unknown defect or isn't retarded in any way. How long do you make this period? Is it two days or two years or when he or she graduates from high school? And what about at the other end of the age spectrum, when someone fails to meet these physical and mental standards? Do you then declare these older Americans nonhumans? You have a real problem when you ignore what science, medicine and biology say about the child in the womb.

31. *The Supreme Court stated, in that Roe v. Wade decision in 1973, that the law protects only legal persons and that "legal personhood does not exist prenatally." Would you agree that, at least for now, it's unimportant*

whether or not the fetus is a human being?

On the contrary, I think what we now know about the human being in the womb will lead to the overturn of *Roe v. Wade*. If you'll remember that on March 6, 1857, in the Dred Scott decision, the Supreme Court of this country ruled that black people were not legal persons either.

32. *The Roe v. Wade decision has stood for almost a decade and a half. What are the chances of it being overturned now?*

Remember it took three Constitutional amendments and a civil war to erase the Dred Scott decision. I would say there is a very good chance that the *Roe* v. *Wade* decision will be reversed in the not too distant future. The issue that has divided our land has divided the court. When the court struck down those abortion regulations in 1986, the vote was 5-4. That's a long way from the 7-2 majority of *Roe* v. *Wade*. Chief Justice Warren Burger even suggested reconsideration of *Roe* v. *Wade* before he resigned, [54] and his replacement, Antonin Scalia, has already displayed opposition to abortion. [55]

33. *Has the Supreme Court ever reversed a major decision?*

Yes, over a hundred times.

34. *Is there any way to get around the Supreme Court if the decision is not reversed?*

Yes, by amending the Constitution. There are two ways this can be accomplished. Both houses of Congress can approve it by a two-thirds vote or a Constitutional Convention can be called by 34 states to approve it. In either case, it would then have to be ratified by three-fourths of the states.

35. *One major difference between the Dred Scott decision and Roe v. Wade is that a fetus is part of a woman's body. How can anyone argue with that?*

The child in the womb cannot be considered part of the mother's body at any stage. A fetus is a complete, separate being from the very beginning, with its own genetic code completely different from the mother's. The fetus has its own blood supply; the type is often different from the mother's. In all organic respects, except from the source of nourishment, the unborn baby is completely separate from the mother.

36. *Yes, except for the nourishment. A woman has the right to her own body. Is it right to make that woman carry or nourish that fetus when she doesn't want to?*

A woman has a right to her own body, but the child in her womb is not part of her own body. Is it right to make a woman responsible for feeding her children outside of the womb when she doesn't feel like it or want to? It's irrelevant, really, because the mother nourishes the baby in her womb automatically. Pregnancy does not incapacitate a woman. She is free to go to school or to work or do any of the things she did before she became pregnant.

37. *There is a certain amount of discomfort associated with pregnancy. While it is possible to work or study, is it fair to make a woman suffer the discomfort associated with pregnancy?*

Discomfort is not a *given* or, if it is, it is not constant. Some women say they felt better during their pregnancy than at any other time of their lives. As for the possible discomfort, I often feel discomfort when I'm tired and don't feel like feeding my child. The extra effort it involves might even give me a headache or make me nauseous. We often must do things we don't feel like doing as a responsible member of society.

38. *But she would have to give birth, and abortion is safer than childbirth. Is it right to make a woman who doesn't want the child suffer the dangers associated with childbirth?*

Abortion is not safer than childbirth. Simple logic would tell us that performing surgery on a healthy woman is likely to increase, not decrease, risk. First, you must know who is providing the statistics. Much of the statistics on abortion today come from the Alan Guttmacher Institute, which is the research arm for Planned Parenthood, the largest provider of abortions in the United States. Even the Supreme Court was fooled when deciding *Roe* v. *Wade* in 1973. It relied on what it called the *established medical fact* that, in the first trimester, maternal mortality in abortion is less than mortality in childbirth. It relied on abortion figures for the first trimester, compared to all pregnancy-related deaths for the full nine months, which included those first trimester abortion deaths. A detailed study on these statistics was published in an anthology, *New Perspectives on Human Abortion* in 1981. Also, other complications, which may occur later, even though directly related to abortion, are often not reported as such.

39. *What do you mean?*

Ectopic or tubal pregnancy has increased over 300 percent since abortion was legalized. [56] (The 400-800 percent figure referred to earlier in this chapter was taken from European studies, where abortion was legalized earlier than it was in the United States.) Scar tissue is formed when the abortionist's curette scrapes or cuts too deeply across the tubes. Then there is no longer enough room for the fertilized ovum to escape. The tube ruptures, and emergency surgery is required. If death occurs, the cause is listed as ectopic pregnancy. [57]

40. *If abortions are outlawed, what would you do with all the unwanted children?*

First of all, how a woman feels about having a child when she first learns she is pregnant and how she feels when she is about to deliver are often quite different. But if a child clearly is not wanted, there are over 2 million couples in the U.S., not to mention other countries, waiting to adopt a baby. The average waiting list for adoption is from three to five years at present.

41. *What about the women who keep these children they really didn't want? Wouldn't this mean an increase in child abuse?*

With that kind of reasoning, child abuse should have declined in this country since *Roe* v. *Wade,* but just the reverse is true. The U.S. Department of Health and Human Services showed a 500 percent increase in cases of child abuse between 1973 and 1982. A landmark study on this was conducted at the University of Southern California by Dr. Edward Lenoski. Ninety-one percent of the 674 battered children he studied were children from planned pregnancies. Their mothers started wearing maternity clothes two months earlier than the control group of nonabused children and the fathers named the boys after themselves 20 percent more often than fathers in the control group.[58] This has been true in all major studies conducted worldwide except two, and both of those studies have been invalidated due to significant differences in the two groups of children studied.

41-A. *What are the two studies that were invalidated?*

Professor Paul Cameron invalidated a study in Sweden by Forssman & Thuwe. Professor Samuel Nigro invalidated a study published in Family Planning Perspectives in 1975.[59]

42. *What about overpopulation and world hunger?*

We certainly don't have an overpopulation problem in this country. For many years now, our birthrate has been below what is necessary to maintain zero population growth. The population of the U.S. is still increasing at present, due to immigration and the fact that people are living longer. In almost every area of the world where there is a problem with hunger today, it is due to political instability, ignorance or unsound religious beliefs. We certainly don't have to resort to killing unborn children to control population.

43. *Suicide has become a big problem. Wouldn't laws against abortion lead to more suicides in women?*

Suicide in pregnant women is extremely rare—much more

common after induced abortion. After one extensive study conducted in the state of Minnesota, researchers found so few suicides in pregnant women compared to the general population that the author concluded that the fetus in utero must be a protective mechanism.[60] Mental trauma following abortion is well documented, however, and can be obtained from American Victims of Abortion, Open Arms or Women Exploited by Abortion. A recent study of long-term manifestions of stress from abortions, published by Dr. Anne C. Speckhard, a Virginia psychologist, revealed that although 72 percent of the women studied claimed they had no religious beliefs at the time of the abortion, 96 percent, in retrospect, regarded their abortion as murder.[61]

44. *I've seen polls where most of the women said they were relieved after having an abortion.*

Many of these polls are taken from questionnaires filled out immediately following an abortion. A group of Canadian psychiatrists found these to be completely unreliable because of the "numbness as a reaction to the trauma or because of repression." Much later, they discovered deep pain and bereavement, coupled with feelings of love for the aborted child.[62]

45. *Don't most Americans support the status quo of legalized abortions?*

No. In a Gallup Poll conducted for *Newsweek Magazine* in 1985, only 21 percent said they felt abortions should be legal under all circumstances, which is what we have now. Some polls are misleading because they only ask the question, "Are you happy with the current abortion law?" Or

"Do you feel that the *Roe* v. *Wade* decision was right?" The truth is that most people don't know what the law is now. Most people are unaware that third trimester abortions are legal or, in fact, legal up to the moment of birth, with no restrictions. In that same Gallup Poll, another 21 percent said that abortions should be illegal in all circumstances, and 55 percent said they should be legal in only certain circumstances. So 76 percent of Americans, whether they know it or not, feel the law should be changed.[63]

46. *What about abortion to save the life of the mother?*

The sacrifice of one life for another has never been illegal. Every pro-life bill or pro-life amendment has always included a provision necessary to save the life of the mother. But let's put that possibility in perspective. The Surgeon General of the United States, Dr. C. Everett Koop, says that "abortion as a necessity to save the life of the mother is so rare as to be almost nonexistent."[64]

47. *If a law prohibiting abortion was passed, how would women be prosecuted?*

They wouldn't, unless one happened to be an abortionist. The mother is really the second victim and needs help and understanding. The abortionists would be prosecuted, as in years past.

48. *Didn't Planned Parenthood run some ads that said, "If you had a miscarriage, you could be prosecuted for murder?"*

More scare tactics by the abortion industry, trying to

imply that women who had miscarriages could be suspected of having induced abortions and prosecuted as such! Show me a woman who has ever been prosecuted for securing an abortion in the history of this country.

49. *What part does Planned Parenthood play in the pro-choice movement?*

In its early years, Planned Parenthood offered contraceptive advice and aid to married women to help them plan their families responsibly. Because of the many years Planned Parenthood spent doing this work, it has enjoyed widespread support as one of the trusted organizations in our country. Also, in its early years, Planned Parenthood specifically opposed abortion. This is from a *Planned Parenthood World Population* brochure, circa 1965: *An abortion kills the life of a baby after it has begun. It is dangerous to your life and health. It may make you sterile so that when you want a child you cannot have it.* [65]

Planned Parenthood has grown to a giant organization, feasting on money from the federal government. According to that organization's 1983 tax return, 60 percent of its total revenues of more than $29.2 million came from federal grants. That same year, Planned Parenthood's own clinics performed 83,000 abortions. [66] So, you see, Planned Parenthood is not just supporting abortion, they're actively involved in the abortion business. Most of Planned Parenthood's clients today are unmarried teenagers.

Planned Parenthood dispenses birth control drugs and devices to these teenagers without parental knowledge or consent. Some of these things, like the pill and the IUD, can be medically hazardous. Planned Parenthood has been actively promoting sex education programs in the schools and elsewhere, which are believed by many to be permissive and to have contributed to increased teenage sexual activity and pregnancy.[67] You will find more information on this subject in my chapter on school-based health clinics.

49-A. *What was wrong with the sex education programs we've had in the public schools since the '60s?*

According to Secretary of Education William J. Bennett and Surgeon General C. Everett Koop, the sex education programs of the past have accepted "children's sexual activity as inevitable" and focused "only on safe sex." In short, they were empty of any sense of right and wrong.[68]

50. *If we make abortions illegal, won't they still go on?*

They will be greatly reduced. There is a relationship between law and behavior in every country. We have laws against many things that still go on. If you follow this line of reasoning, then perhaps we should decriminalize rape. Then we could use tax money to buy the rapist a clean hotel room where he could commit his crime because, after all, it's going to go on anyway. Passing a law never completely eliminates any problem. It merely gives us some control over it.

51. *Wouldn't passing a law making abortions illegal discriminate against poor women because the rich will be able to obtain them anyway?*

That's like saying if poor people can't afford all the drugs they want, we should buy them and distribute them to everyone. It is true; the rich have always been able to afford more vices.

52. *While we're on the subject of law and order, what about all the violence that has been brought about by the pro-life movement at abortion clinics?*

I don't know of any pro-life organization that condones violence. To use the words of Joe Scheidler of the Pro-Life Action League, "The use of violence would only reinforce the erroneous belief that the end justifies the means—that evil can be overcome by evil. This is the abortionist's mentality, not ours."[69]

53. *If the pro-life movement does not condone those clinic bombings, you must agree that they are responsible because they are the ones that have been keeping people stirred up over this issue.*

You are right, there are a lot of people stirred up over this issue, but with over 1,500,000 abortions a year in this country, you are bound to get a few people who are so emotional they may react foolishly. They're more likely to be stirred up because their daughter or wife or a good friend was maimed in one of those clinics, rather than by people who are picketing on the street, counseling women and giving out pro-life literature.

54. *But isn't it wrong to let those picketers harass the women who are going in for abortions?*

They do not harass them; all they do is tell those women who will listen what the truth is about the abortion procedure and about their pregnancy, and offer them help. They also tell them where they can get a free pregnancy test, because many of these abortion clinics have been investigated and some have been found guilty of doing abortions on women who aren't even pregnant.[70]

55. *Some say the abortion issue is a question of relative values. If you're going to have a society in which fetal life is absolutely sacrosanct, can women ever be free and equal human beings if they are going to be vulnerable to the biological process of procreation while men are not?*

Men are vulnerable in other ways and, although feminists don't like to admit it, men do assume most of the financial responsibility for the family, in most circumstances. This is not the law—those laws have been removed—but it is fact. It's true that men can't biologically have children, but most women today feel that childbearing is a privilege, not a burden. Women can and, in fact, do perform almost any job performed by men, but no attempt to make men and women equal can make us identical. In fact, bearing a child is something a man definitely cannot do.

56. *But can you have equality without control of fertility? It's the cornerstone of women's freedom.*

Women will never completely stop being victims until they stop victimizing others—the weak, innocent, unborn. You cannot enhance a woman's rights by denying the most basic right of all to her unborn daughter.

57. *What if she's carrying a son?*

Well, about half the time it's a girl. It is sad, but true, that more and more children are being aborted in this country simply because they are not the sex desired by the couple.[71] It is perfectly legal and, more often than not, the child that is aborted is female.

58. But abortion is often a young girl's first step to self-assertion.

I don't think abortions are any way to build self-esteem or self-confidence in young girls. If you'll contact some of the organizations that exist to help abortion victims, they'll tell you that this simply is not the case.

59. Do you admit that teenage pregnancy brings great hardship and suffering?

Show me someone who has never suffered and I'll show you someone who has never lived. A teenage girl may suffer some in the few months while she is waiting for her child to be born, but she can also use this time to learn and to improve her life if she'll contact some of the organizations who are out there waiting to help her. She would likely suffer much, much more if she finds she can't have children later because some abortionist has damaged and stretched the muscles in her uterus.

60. But doesn't a woman have the right to control her own body?

Yes, but not someone else's. The baby she is carrying is not her own body. May I suggest that if she did control her own body at the appropriate time, she would not be subject to an unplanned pregnancy.

61. How do you answer the charges that the pro-life move-

ment is against contraception, child-care services and child welfare?

I don't know of many pro-life organizations that take a stand on contraception before a pregnancy occurs. The Catholic organizations do because artificial contraception violates their religious beliefs. But do you really think you are going to get the people in this country to be more concerned about child welfare by trivializing conception and pregnancy?

62. *What advice would you give a young girl whose parents or pastor counsel her to get an abortion?*

I would tell her to seek help through her local Crisis Pregnancy Center or pro-life organization. There are over 2,000 of these organizations in North America. Through these groups, volunteers are ready to give any type of help that is needed, including counseling for parents. No one can be forced to get an abortion against her will.

(If you are discussing this question with someone who believes in God and in the Bible, you can reinforce your answer with the following statements:)

The Bible tells us to honor our father and mother and to respect our spiritual authority, but not if they are asking us to do something that contradicts Scripture. Remember, this may seem like an easy out, but God knows our hearts. Each of us must take responsibility for our own decisions.

63. *How would you solve the abortion problem?*

I would support a human life amendment that would guarantee the sanctity of life, not only for the unborn, but also for the elderly and the handicapped. I would urge women to take another look at the bill of goods we've been sold by the abortion industry, and realize it's a half-billion-dollar-a-year industry interested in only one thing—making a profit!

An uninformed choice is really no choice at all. We communicate by satellite, perform surgery with lasers and put people on the moon. Surely we can solve our social problems without resorting to violence. Abortion is a matter of *right*, not *rights*.

5

Isn't Everyone For Equal Rights?

Amending the Constitution of the United States is not an easy matter. It takes approval by two-thirds of each house of Congress to propose an amendment. Then it must be ratified by three-fourths of the states within a seven-year period.

The process was not designed to be a simple one because, once an amendment is ratified and placed in the Constitution, it's the law of the land and cannot be changed by a simple act of Congress or a state legislature. Our forefathers went to great lengths to insure there would be time for proper debate and study before any changes could be made that might affect the rights and liberties that so many had fought and died to secure. The battle over the Equal Rights Amendment is our latest illustration of the need for such an involved process.

History

The women's liberation movement captured the nation's attention in the early '70s. The Ninety-second

Congress approved the new Equal Rights Amendment by an overwhelming margin of 354-23 in the House of Representatives on October 12, 1971, and by 84-9 in the Senate on March 22, 1972. The states were poised to follow suit. Hawaii rushed it through within hours after congressional approval, and the other states were practically falling all over each other to get in line. Fourteen states approved it within the first month and 30 within the first year—all with little or no debate. With only eight states to go, the ERA appeared a shoo-in as the Twenty-seventh Amendment to our Constitution.

By the end of 1972, however, the nation's best and brightest constitutional lawyers, researchers and scholars had begun to share the results of their studies on the proposed amendment. Phyllis Schlafly, the outspoken president of Eagle Forum, founded and became national chairman of *Stop ERA*. Mrs. Schlafly crisscrossed the country in an effort to educate the public on the drawbacks and possible negative effects of the ERA, and successfully put the brakes on the ERA bandwagon. In the six years that followed, only five more states chose to ratify the amendment, bringing the total to 35, three short of the necessary 38.

In 1978, in an unprecedented last-ditch attempt to salvage the ERA, Congress voted to extend the seven-year deadline by three years and three months. About that time, Beverly LaHaye founded *Concerned Women for America* (CWA), which joined Phyllis Schlafly in the effort to educate the American public on the ERA. Not a single state ratified the ERA during that controversial extension period and, by the time the new deadline rolled around in 1982, five states were attempting to withdraw their approval.

The controversy surrounding the ERA was not, and is not, about granting women equal rights, but whether the 52 words of the ERA are the appropriate way of achieving that objective. The debate that normally follows any proposed constitutional amendment concerns whether or not the end result would be desirable, but the language of the ERA is so broad that this debate has centered around just what the end results of this proposed amendment would be.

For example, the debate that occurred when the Nineteenth Amendment (women's suffrage) was proposed was over whether or not it was desirable to give women the right to vote. Everybody knew what the end result would be before it was passed. The ERA arguments have not been over whether or not women should be in combat, but whether women will be placed in combat by the ERA; not whether homosexual marriages should be legalized, but whether the ERA will legalize homosexual marriages; not whether public funding should be used for abortions, but whether the ERA will mandate public funds be used for abortions; and not whether common sense exceptions will remain a part of our law, but whether the ERA will permit common sense exceptions to allow for personal privacy and physical differences.

That last item causes a great amount of concern among most ERA opponents. If common sense exceptions are permitted (we have no way of knowing with the present language of the ERA), then we have no way of knowing what they will be. But, if they are allowed, they will be decided, not by our elected representatives who are responsible to the people, but by federal judges appointed for life. Since all these facts have been brought to light, the majority of our nation's lawmakers have been unwilling to approve the ERA, with its broad-sweeping language, a second time. It would be like asking the women in America to take an experimental drug and saying, "It might help you, but there are some uncertain side effects."

But the ERA and the controversy surrounding it are far from over. The National Organization for Women (NOW) will not let it die. According to NOW president Eleanor Smeal, the amendment is the number one fundraiser, the single cause that rallies and recruits activists across the age spectrum. It draws women in.[1]

The major carrot at the end of the NOW stick is the promise of equal pay for equal work. This already is law. Furthermore, constitutional law is for the sole purpose of regulating and controlling the power of the government. It does not, and cannot, regulate acts by private employers and businesses.

Through the efforts of Eleanor Smeal and NOW, the ERA has been reintroduced in Congress with every new session as Senate Joint Resolution 1 in an attempt to get it approved so that the ratification process can begin all over again. In addition, NOW has renewed its effort to pass state ERAs, carefully targeting those states in liberal areas. Victories on the state level would be used as fuel for a renewed federal campaign.

On the positive side, this controversy has created a near unanimous consensus among all Americans for equal rights for women. The ERA debate focused the nation's attention on injustices that existed in national and state laws for men and women, and most have been eliminated. Those that remain fall into one of four basic categories:

> 1. Laws that are trivial and are biased only in the sense that they do not employ *sex-*

neutral terms such as *chairperson.*

2. Laws that have nothing to do with genuine discrimination in the sense that laws on prostitution or abortion generally can apply only to women.

3. Laws that are so clearly archaic and out of date that nobody pays them any serious attention. They should be repealed, but have not been because they are ignored. For example, an old law in Spokane, Washington, prohibited women from working in fruit stands.

4. Laws that do differentiate between men and women and do so properly in the view of most people. Such laws include some relating to military combat, marriage, criminal sex offenses and personal privacy.[2]

Another by-product of this debate is that a number of laws that were created especially to protect women have also been eliminated. A law establishing a maximum lifting capacity is an example of a protective labor law.

If you're going to discuss the ERA, the first thing you must know is the wording—the exact wording. Memorize the following three sections before going any further.

Equal Rights Amendment

Section 1. Equality of rights under the law shall not be denied or abridged by the United States or by any State on account of sex.

Section 2. The Congress shall have the power to enforce by appropriate legislation the provisions of this article.

Section 3. This amendment shall take effect two years after the date of ratification.

Public opinion polls continue to reflect widespread support for the ERA. This indicates that we've done a better job educating our lawmakers than we have the general public. Since our legislative representatives should—and do—listen to the will of the people we must complete the educational process.

A WORD OF CAUTION

The biggest obstacle we have in educating the public on this issue is the name of the amendment—the Equal Rights Amendment. People automatically assume that if you are against it, you are against equal rights for women. For this reason I recommend using the initials—ERA— and humor—whenever possible.

Also, avoid bringing up the issue of unisex bathrooms. Although there is room for concern in this area, if you bring up unisex bathrooms, the other side will make fun of you and pass it off as ridiculous, and you automatically lose. If you find yourself in a debate and someone on your side brings up unisex bathrooms, switch the discussion to one on whether common sense exceptions, based on physical differences between the sexes, will be allowed with the present ERA wording. Except to extremists on both sides, this common sense standard represents responsible public policy.

QUESTIONS AND ANSWERS

1. *What is your position on the ERA?*

I think it's an excellent way to compare baseball pitchers, a pretty good laundry detergent and a poor constitutional amendment.

2. *Why would the ERA be a poor constitutional amendment?*

Because the ERA is essentially a prohibition, one that allows no distinctions between men and women, boys and girls, no matter how necessary or reasonable they may be.

2-A. *What distinctions do you feel are necessary?*

Distinctions based on biological and physiological differences.

2-B. *Why would distinctions based on biological and physiological differences be necessary?*

Most people recognize the need for personal privacy between the sexes. Also, some jobs require certain physical requirements, such as those of police officers and firefighters.

2-C. *You must acknowledge that many women already have met the physical requirements for police officers and firefighters.*

Yes, but it is also true that, in these jobs, some long established physical requirements are being relaxed to afford more women opportunities; however, with the ERA, where physical requirements lead to *under-representation*, the standards would have to be dropped even further. This would greatly reduce the effectiveness of these forces and put people who are in need of these services in jeopardy.

3. *Can you name a job that requires a particular set of genitals?*

Not one that I think should be legalized! But I can name many jobs where certain physical or mental abilities which are more common to one or the other of the sexes are required.

4. *Can you give an example?*

Yes. Piano tuners are virtually all males. The difference in the development of the male and female brain, which occurs between the sixteenth and twenty-sixth week of life, gives some males this special ability. (You can use differences in strength here, giving the firefighter example, but this one should throw them off balance if they're trying to use the argument that there are no other important differences between the sexes.)[3]

4-A. *What is this difference in brain development?*

There is a chemical bath, which is given to the left side of the male brain and the connecting cord, that has to do with how the different sexes process information.[4]

4-B. *Are you saying that the male brain is superior?*

Not at all; but the male and female brains do operate differently. The left hemisphere of the male brain often shrinks during that chemical bath, and some of the connecting tissue is destroyed. This gives some areas of specialization to the male brain, but also reduces the ability for lateral transmission between the brain's hemispheres.[5] The important thing to remember is that, just as there are differences in strength between men and women, there are other intrinsic physiological differences that make one sex better suited to certain jobs than the other.

5. *Do you feel the sexes are equal?*

We are equal, but not identical! You must remember, I am not against equal rights for women, but simply the language of the ERA.

6. *What's wrong with letting a woman do a job, if she can handle it, that you say is better suited to a man?*

Not a thing, but recent civil rights history repeatedly shows that where eligibility standards fail to result in representative proportions, the standards are relaxed. If the ERA passed, then, in jobs such as firefighting, the government would not be able to hire only the qualified women; they would be forced to relax the standards. For instance, if women cannot drag a 200-pound body for 100 yards, the requirement might be lowered to a 150-pound body for 50 yards. This could result in a loss of lives.

7. *How would you ensure that women have equal opportunities in employment without the ERA?*

Women are already guaranteed equal opportunity in employment by the Equal Employment Opportunity Act of 1972.

7-A. *According to the Civil Rights Commission, there are loopholes in the Equal Employment Opportunity Act that the ERA would solve.*

The Commission objects to providing employment opportunities limited to a single sex where there exists what is called a *bona fide occupational requirement.* This would include a job as a housemother in a college girl's dorm or a job as a shoe-shine attendant in a male bathroom. Most Americans feel these are normal and reasonable exceptions.

7-B. *The Equal Employment Opportunity Act also applies only to employers with 15 or more employees.*

If this act is too weak, it can be amended by a simple act of Congress.

8. *How would you solve the problem of equal pay for equal work?*

Equal pay for equal work is already the law of the land. It is covered in the Equal Pay Act of 1963 and the Civil Rights Acts of 1964, among others.

9. *But women are still discriminated against in this area.*

This is unfortunate, but true. We have laws on the books against murder and there are people who murder. Laws of any kind must be continually enforced. Cases of wage discrimination can be remedied by your local Equal Employment Opportunity Commission or through civil lawsuits. Lawyers love this type of case because it's an automatic win.

10. *Why not just pass the ERA and do away with all types of discrimination once and for all?*

Because the ERA will not solve these problems. First and foremost, a constitutional amendment only regulates and controls the power of the government. It has no power over private employers and private business at all.

11. *Wouldn't it at least be a step in the right direction to pass the ERA and control discrimination in federal and state laws?*

The Equal Protection Clause of the Fourteenth Amendment already covers this. It states: *No person shall be denied the equal protection of the laws.*

12. *But aren't the standards for evaluating sex discrimination under the Fourteenth Amendment less strict than those for evaluating other kinds of discrimination?*

This is true. The Equal Protection Clause of the Fourteenth Amendment prohibits disparate treatment between men and women when they are *similarly situated.* In other words, it allows common sense exceptions when they are based upon physical differences or when they grow out of the need for personal privacy between the sexes.

13. *What about pension discrimination?*

It is true that women often pay more for pension plans and

life insurance because statistics show, on an average, they live longer than men; however, women pay less for automobile insurance because they are found to be safer drivers in almost every category of miles driven. In some areas that have state ERAs, gender is not allowed in figuring insurance rates. This tends to be a hardship for poor women because employers tend to pay for life insurance and pension plans, while the cost of automobile insurance is borne by the individual.

14. *What about discrimination that exists in divorce laws?*

A good many divorce laws have granted special protection to a wife and mother. Many of these have been struck down and many older women, who have devoted years to raising and caring for their families, have suffered. Of those that remain, most draw unnecessary and archaic distinctions, which could be overturned, if necessary, under present statutory law or the Fourteenth Amendment.

14-A. *What do you mean by if necessary?*

Most laws of this type are simply ignored, but overturning them could be an interesting hobby. When someone questions you about laws that discriminate in areas with which you are not familiar, request that he or she state the law, and then compare that law to one of the four types of alleged discrimination laws still on the books, which I mentioned in the introduction to this section. Some of these laws are so ridiculous you can just repeat them and then say, "I rest my case," or "Do you really want to waste time commenting on that?" Don't forget to use humor when appropriate.

15. *But isn't the ERA necessary to put women in the Constitution?*

The word *women* or *woman* is not mentioned in the ERA. It says *on account of sex*. In fact, some ERA supporters have stated they would be more comfortable if, instead of *sex*, the ERA said *gender*.

15-A. *Why would it be important to switch sex to gender?*

Some feel the wording would then apply more directly to male and female. Many constitutional experts have testified that the present wording of the ERA could legalize homosexual marriages and make it illegal to discriminate against homosexual couples wishing to adopt children.

16. *Would the ERA legalize homosexual marriage?*

With the present wording, we have no way of knowing before it is passed. It would be open to interpretation by the courts. A hundred years ago, no one would have dreamed that the First Amendment would protect pornography. Gay rights groups are marching right along with the National Organization for Women, and NOW proudly proclaims that gay and lesbian rights are one of that organization's primary concerns.

17. *What criminal laws would be affected?*

Laws forbidding various forms of homosexual conduct likely would be disallowed.[6] Also, laws that apply only to a single sex or unequally to one sex—such as in rape or prostitution—would be vulnerable. The ERA's primary proponent, the National Organization for Women, already has approved a resolution to support legislation to decriminalize the voluntary aspects of adult prostitution.[7]

18. Would the ERA have any effect on the abortion issue?

It could guarantee abortion funding. The question already
has been raised in four states that have ERAs. Hawaii
dumped out on procedural grounds. Massachusetts'
courts demanded funding, but did not use the ERA in
deciding the case. In Pennsylvania, an intermediate judge
said yes, but it was overturned in a higher court; and abortion funding was upheld by a Connecticut state trial judge,
and the state's attorney general refused to appeal. To
date, two states have gotten down to the question and
split.

19. Would the ERA place women in combat?

According to the Yale Law Journal, "The Equal Rights
Amendment will have a substantial and pervasive impact
upon military practices and institutions. As now formu-
lated, the Amendment permits no exceptions for the military."[8]

19-A. What would be wrong in assigning qualified women to combat duty?

(See firefighting example in question 6.) If the ERA is
passed, the standards may have to be lowered to allow an
equal number of men and women to qualify for combat
duty. But even if the standards are maintained, in a
national emergency, there could be significant problems
created in weeding out those who could not qualify, if men
and women were drafted into the military on an equal
basis.

19-B. *The Soviet Union and Israel have women in the military.*

Both countries have abandoned the practice of using women in combat; in Israel, it was because of what the other side did to the Israeli women on the front lines in the war of 1948. Also, the women in Israel today are assigned only one-half of the service time of the men.

20. *Aren't you really forgetting that common sense has to be employed in the process of interpreting the ERA relating to combat, strength and personal privacy between the sexes?*

The common sense standard is precisely what we have today under the Fourteenth Amendment, and that is what is so disliked by many ERA proponents. The courts will always assume that the intent of a new constitutional amendment is to change the law. Also, it is likely the court would look into amendments that were rejected during the congressional debate over the issues to gain a clearer understanding of the intent of the legislators who proposed the amendment. Those rejected amendments include: laws relating to compulsory military service or combat service; protective labor laws; laws that extend protection to wives, mothers or widows; laws that impose family support obligations upon the husband; laws that promote privacy for men or women, or boys or girls; laws relating to punishment for sex offenses; and laws based upon physiological or functional differences between men and women.

20-A. *What about the constitutional right to privacy?*

*Wouldn't that protect us from being roomed in coedu-
cational dorms or the like?*

There is nothing in the language of the Constitution that
refers to any *right to privacy*. A handful of Supreme Court
justices pulled that out of the hat in 1973 to justify the right
to abortion. It is still a matter of disagreement among the
justices, and has never been fully articulated in any decision of the high court. It represents no more than a hope.
It is certainly not a barrier we can rely on to protect us
from abuse in ERA interpretation.

20-B. *You must admit that, since the Supreme Court used
the right to privacy in the matter of abortion, it's
highly likely the Court will use it again in interpreting the ERA.*

If, in fact there is a privacy doctrine, it appears it would be
amended by the Equal Rights Amendment, not the other
way around. It is a common sense rule of constitutional
interpretation that the provision that comes later in time
takes precedence.[9]

21. *What effect would the ERA have on labor laws?*

Affirmative action programs, designed to give preference
to women in hiring and in college admission programs,
would be called into question. Any remaining laws, created
to protect women in the work place, likely would be found
unconstitutional if the ERA should pass. For instance,
women in manual labor jobs could not be protected with
laws such as those regulating maximum lifting capacity.
Also, employment seniority systems may be called into
question because workers with most seniority are usually
men.

22. Would the ERA have any effect on churches?

Many churches—Catholic, Mormon, and Orthodox Jewish synagogues, to name a few—deny various rights and positions to women. There is reason to doubt these religious institutions would be allowed to retain their tax-exempt status if the ERA passed.

22-A. Wouldn't freedom of religion prevail?

The Internal Revenue Service already has succeeded in having the tax-exempt status of Bob Jones University removed, so, obviously, freedom of religion does not always prevail.

22-B. Doesn't the Bible teach that man is superior to woman?

No, the Bible says in 1 Corinthians 11:11,12: "In the Lord . . . woman is not independent of man, nor is man independent of woman. For as woman came from man, so also man is born of woman. But everything comes from God." The Bible does refer to certain practices in the Church that followed the accepted customs of the time, and they must be viewed in that light. Many times an understanding of the customs of the day can make the difference of correct or incorrect interpretation of the Bible. Another important thing to remember in understanding Scripture is that it must not be taken out of context, and that Scripture does not contradict Scripture. Although there are divisions among denominations as to which practices must be observed in the Church, the Bible does not say that woman is unequal or of lesser importance than man.

22-C. *But doesn't the Bible tell the wife to submit to the husband?*

Yes, but again, you must not take it out of context. If all of the conditions for husbands and wives listed in Ephesians 5 were observed, there would be no problems in marriage. You must remember that it was God who originally ordained marriage and He gave us certain practical ground rules that, if followed, will make a marriage work.

22-D. *Does this mean that women are to submit to all men?*

No, that would be ridiculous. You must also remember that a woman does not have to get married. A single woman's only responsibility is to God.

23. *Would the ERA affect other private institutions?*

Most likely it would result in greater governmental intrusion in private schools, clubs and organizations. In 1976, the Supreme Court ruled that strictly private schools, including those with no government assistance, were prohibited from discriminating on the basis of race. Gender classifications are judged by a slightly different standard now, but the ERA would change that, and we could expect the end of not only single-sex schools and organizations, but groups such as the Boy Scouts and Girl Scouts as well.

23-A. *Why should racial and gender classifications be treated differently?*

Because there is no need for common sense exceptions, based on the need for personal privacy and physical differences between races.

24. *How would the ERA affect women in athletics?*

Unisex teams in high schools and colleges would undoubtedly be the law of the land for schools that receive public funds. Girls have already won the right to play on boys' football teams in at least three states—Pennsylvania, Washington and Texas. The same law would have to be applied to allow boys on girls' teams, or abolish boys' teams altogether. This would result in fewer opportunities for women in sports, or else the rules of contact sports would have to be changed to assure representative proportions.

25. *Let's look at the states with ERAs. We have a few girls playing on boys' high school athletic teams. What other changes have state ERAs brought about?*

Women have lost existing advantages in divorce and child custody cases. Virtually all gains could be or, in fact, have been won using the more traditional equal protection laws.

26. *Haven't state ERAs really proved there is nothing to fear from having the ERA as part of the Constitution?*

No, for three big reasons. One, most of these state provisions use different language from that of the ERA. Remember, it's not the concept of equal rights that is being debated, but the language of the ERA. Two, state judges, who are often elected and more accountable to the people and sensitive to the needs of their specific areas, are interpreting the state ERAs. And, three, there has been very little litigation involving feminist demands, because the feminists are concerned now about not raising issues that will be detrimental to getting the federal ERA passed.

27. *Wouldn't it be best to pass the ERA and let the courts decide?*

If someone asked you to take a new drug that was experimental because it might help you, but added that there are unknown side effects, would you take it? Of course not! We've never intentionally placed anything in the document that serves as the supreme law of our land without knowing what the specific results would be. This would be an act of irresponsibility.

28. *What is your solution to this problem of equal rights for women?*

First, I would urge women everywhere to acknowledge that we already have the laws on the books to guarantee those rights. A cure is of no use if you won't acknowledge the cure and take the pill. We must not remain shackled by the hurts of the past. We must not waste time with a worthless piece of legislation that surely will bring about unwanted and divisive side effects, and waste the time of our courts.

Second, I would bring men back into the dialogue and see them as part of the solution, not the problem.

Third, I would call on committed women and men everywhere to work toward seeing these laws fully explored and vigorously enforced.

And, finally, I would call on women leaders who have backed the ERA in the past to study all the findings, be courageous, join some of their colleagues and elected representatives who have changed their minds on this issue, admit that the ERA is a mistake and place it on the garbage heap where it belongs. Then, together, we can go forward!

6

JUST WHAT EXACTLY IS PORNOGRAPHY?

Therefore God gave them over in the sinful desires of their hearts to sexual impurity for the degrading of their bodies with one another (Rom. 1:24).

Pornography is harmless. It's not a social problem. It may even have a beneficial effect and should be free from regulation and control. It's a relatively small industry and, if ignored, people will get bored and lose interest, and it will go away.

Those were essentially the findings of the 1970 Presidential Commission on Obscenity and Pornography!

JUST HOW BAD IS IT?

In 1970, this *relatively small* industry grossed around $1 billion. Now it's $8 billion.[1] That's nearly $22 million a day, $900,000 an hour or $15,000 every minute. Eighty-

five percent of that money goes into the pockets of organized crime;[2] much is untaxed.[3]

The 1970 commission was right about one thing. People did get bored and lose interest. There is no longer a
demand for what was available in 1970, and so some of it
did go away. The simple nudity and even consenting sexual
intercourse between the man and woman of yesterday
have been replaced by violent and sadistic acts performed
on women and children, explicit group sex, explicit oral
and anal intercourse, sex between people and all types of
animals, sadomasochism, violent homosexual and lesbian
activity, urination, defecation, enemas, rape, torture, cutting of genitals and even death. In *snuff* films, the model is
coerced into performing various sexual acts and then
appears to be murdered before the cameras.

KIDDIE PORN

The 1970 commission nowhere mentioned nor alluded
to child pornography, but their recommendations included
repeal of all laws restraining distribution of sexually
explicit materials to children.[4] In 1973, the first child *porn*
ring was uncovered and, in the years that followed, *kiddie
porn* flourished. In 1977, a full-scale congressional investi-
gation was held. According to the evidence at the hearings, those industries were producing some 264 commercial magazines each month showing children nude or
engaged in sexual conduct. The founder of the Los
Angeles Sexually Exploited Child Unit reported that there
were over 30,000 sexually exploited children in that city
alone.[5]

How does child pornography begin? With pornography.
The offender introduces his victim to pornography for sex

education. Child porn is used to convince the victim that other children are sexually active, so it's okay. The resistance is lowered and, when the sessions progress to sexual activity, more pictures are taken. The pictures are used to control the victims and to introduce other children to sex. The vicious circle is complete.[6]

> It would be better for him to be thrown into the sea with a millstone tied around his neck than for him to cause one of these little ones to sin (Luke 17:2).

The 1977 Protection of Children from Sexual Exploitation Act and the 1984 Child Protection Act have forced the industry underground and under the counter, but recent testimony in the hearings of the Attorney General's Commission on Pornography revealed that kiddie porn is still a thriving industry. Photo sets and videos are bought, sold and traded through the mail[7] and through computer networks.[8]

Those who maintain that pornography is a victimless crime have ignored the young who fall into the hands of vicious exploiters. The American Civil Liberties Union acknowledges that kiddie porn production is a crime; however, once it's produced, the ACLU insists it should not be illegal for someone to own, sell or distribute child pornography.[9] The 1970 Presidential Commission on Obscenity and Pornography chairman and executive director were both leaders in the American Civil Liberties Union.

THE FINDINGS OF THE NEW COMMISSION

On May 20, 1985, Attorney General Edwin Meese

announced the formation of the new Commission on Pornography. He assembled a diverse 11-member panel to investigate changes that had occurred over the last several years. He asked the panel to study the nature, volume and impact of new technology. They were charged with the responsibility of making specific recommendations concerning more effective ways to contain the spread of pornography, consistent with the Constitution.

The Commission worked tirelessly over the next 14 months, holding lengthy hearings in six states, reviewing 2,375 magazines, 725 books and 2,370 films. On July 3, 1986, a two-volume, 1,960-page study was released. That study included 92 recommendations aimed at officials from the White House to local health authorities and to the general public—that's you and me. This sharply divided group agreed that, "The available evidence strongly supports the hypothesis that substantial exposure to sexually violent materials as described here bears a causal [not casual] relation to antisocial acts of sexual violence and, for some subgroups, possibly to unlawful acts of sexual violence."[10] Further, it concluded that "substantial exposure to material of this type will increase acceptance of the proposition that women like to be forced into sexual practices, and once again, that the woman who says no really means yes."[11]

The commission gave three main reasons for the growth of the industry: (1) organized crime, (2) failure of law enforcement, and (3) citizen apathy. On the surface, that's bad news, but let's examine these things one by one.

"The Mafia has really done us a favor," the commission's executive director, Alan Sears, said. "They've eliminated all the competition. We know who almost all the major distributors are. We know where they live and what kind of cars they drive. I know their attorneys personally." Sears claims that if the order to enforce the laws already on the books is handed down from the top, the problem can be eliminated rather quickly. "They're like apples on a tree waiting to be picked."[12]

In October, 1986, three months after the commission's *Final Report* was officially released and five months after it was delivered to his staff, the attorney general accepted the challenge issued by the commission and created the Obscenity Enforcement Unit.

A SINISTER PLAN

Why did it take so long? Syndicated columnist Mike McManus revealed a sinister plan launched by Gray & Company, the largest public relations firm in Washington, to discredit the commission a full month before the report was issued. Grey & Company was hired by "Media Coalition," which includes magazine and book publishers and their distributors, with a budget not to exceed $900,000. McManus shared the details of this plan in his introduction to a special edition of *The Final Report of the Attorney General's Commission on Pornography,* published by Rutledge Hill.[13] The full report is available from the Government Printing Office for $35. The Rutledge Hill edition is being distributed at around $10 in an effort to get this important information into the hands of the people. It can be found in Christian bookstores. The introduction by McManus is a useful guide to this lengthy document.

The plan appeared to be followed to the letter, as news stories of the release of the *Final Report* contained these recurring themes: no scientific basis; a waste of the nation's time, energy, and so on; and a campaign by *religious extremists* to infringe on others' rights.

The Public Didn't Buy It!

The citizens of this country had had enough and began flooding the nation's capitol with cards and letters and tying up phone lines demanding action. Members of organizations such as the National Federation for Decency and Concerned Women for America were in the forefront of a campaign that led companies like Revco, Peoples Drug and 7-Eleven to pull *Playboy* and *Penthouse* off their shelves.

The summer before that, a group of Washington wives had organized the Parents Music Resource Center to fight rock music lyrics and videos containing explicit sex, violence and substance abuse. On November 1, 1985, the organization forced the music industry to agree to place warning labels or printed lyrics on LPs containing these messages.[14]

Were these simply the first blows by the American people who wanted to lash out at an obscenity invasion now in our very homes via cable TV and *Dial-A-Porn?* On July 25, some highly placed religious leaders, who had remained strangely silent on this issue, assembled on the steps of St. Patrick's Cathedral in New York City to endorse the commission's top priorities. It was a momentous occasion, causing Pornography Commissioner, Father Bruce Ritter, to assess this meeting of the heads of every major denomination representing 150 million people (86 percent of the adult population) as *more important* than the commission's report, because it *mainstreamed* the conclusion that pornography is harmful."[15] Yet the event was not covered by the three major networks nor the three leading news magazines.

Not since the beginning of our history have this nation's religious leaders and their followers been so united on an issue. A recent Gallup poll showed that 76 percent of the American people want a total ban on magazines and movies that show sexual violence, and only 4 to 6 percent feel there should be no restrictions whatsoever.[16]

The Attorney General's commission made no recommendation for major changes in the law, but urged that existing laws be conscientiously enforced. The commission concerned itself with that which was criminally obscene (see question-and-answer section for definitions). Perhaps one of the most valuable segments of the report was aimed at you and me: "Suggestions for Citizen and Community Action and Corporate Responsibility." It contains a step-by-step guide to fight not only that which is criminally obscene, but that which is legal but offensive.[17]

Though magazines such as *Playboy*, *Penthouse* and *Hustler* do not fit the legal definition of obscenity because they do not portray ultimate sexual acts explicitly, the commission's *Final Report* stated that a "fairly strong correlation was found between these circulation rates and rape rates."[18] Dr. Judith Reisman, former producer of the popular children's TV program "Captain Kangaroo," aided by a team of 19 researchers, conducted a 1985 Justice Department-funded study of 683 issues of these magazines. Altogether, the coders identified 2,016 child cartoons and 3,988 child visuals. The age most often depicted was 6-11, the most common years of child sexual abuse. Dr. Reisman presented her findings to the commission in November of 1985. According to Dr. Reisman, "These and other examples give evidence of specific attempts to titillate the readers' desire for children as sex stimuli."[19]

CAUSE FOR ALARM

Statistics say that one out of three 12-year-old girls in this country will be the victim of a violent crime in her life-time.[20] Can we allow this to happen? Can we, as Christians, sit back and do nothing?

Anyone, then, who knows the good he ought to do and doesn't do it, sins (Jas. 4:17).

Can we keep the pressure on long enough to eliminate this powerful blight on our society? Citizens in Atlanta, Cincinnati and Arlington, Virginia have completely rid their cities of hard-core pornography. The Attorney General's Commission on Pornography has given us a road map to clean up the rest of the country, and has placed the burden of the responsibility on the attorney general, on the justice system, and on you and me.

But each one is tempted when, by his own evil desire, he is dragged away and enticed. Then, after desire has conceived, it gives birth to sin; and sin, when it is full-grown, gives birth to death (Jas. 1:14,15).

QUESTIONS AND ANSWERS

1. *What is pornography?*

The working definition given us by the Attorney General's

Commission on Pornography states that it is material which "is predominantly sexually explicit and intended primarily for the purpose of sexual arousal."

2. What is hard-core pornography?

Material that is sexually explicit to the extreme, intended virtually and exclusively to arouse, and devoid of any other apparent content or purpose.

3. What is obscenity?

Obscenity was defined by the Supreme Court in *Miller* v. *California* in 1973. According to that definition, material is obscene if it meets this three-pronged test:

a. Whether the average person, applying contemporary community standards would find that the work, taken as a whole, appeals to the prurient [lustful] interest.
b. Whether the work depicts or describes, in a patently offensive way, sexual conduct specifically defined by the applicable state law, and
c. Whether the work, taken as a whole, lacks serious literary, artistic, political, or scientific value.

The Supreme Court gave examples of the second prong of the test. They include:

Patently offensive representations or descriptions of ultimate sexual acts, normal or perverted, actual or simulated; and
Patently offensive representations or descriptions

of masturbation, excretory functions, and lewd exhibition of the genitals.[21]

4. What is child pornography?

Real children, really being photographed and really being molested. It's against the law in almost every state, and it's against the law federally to distribute it across state lines.

5. Doesn't the First Amendment protect pornography under freedom of speech?

The Supreme Court does not define hard-core pornography or obscenity as speech. The Court has said several times that obscenity, like libel and slander, is a crime not protected by the First Amendment.

6. But you can't legislate morality.

Every law legislates morality. Every law sets standards for behavior based on someone's morals.

7. Isn't it censorship to say what someone can and cannot buy?

Censorship is the prior restraint by government of publication. After it's published, it's subject to the scrutiny of the law. Part three of the *Miller v. California* test prevents censorship after publication. Does it have literary, artistic, political or scientific value? That's what keeps people from pulling out library books or any other work of worth.

8. What was the finding of the Attorney General's Commis-

sion on Pornography, released in July of 1986?

That exposure to sexually violent materials increases the likelihood of aggression against women and children and that it perpetrates the myth that women want to be abused and raped. The second category studied—sexual activity without violence but containing degradation, submission, humiliation and dominance—also was found harmful in many ways. The commission found that the industry is controlled largely by organized crime, that the spread of obscenity must be stopped, that we have the laws on the books to eradicate obscenity, but they have not been vigorously enforced.

9. *Didn't two of the commissioners change their minds after the final meeting?*

Yes. Becker and Levine, in their personal statements, said, "The social science research has not been designed to evaluate the relationship between exposure to pornography and the commission of sexual crimes."[22] However, a group of the nation's leading social scientists met with Surgeon General C. Everett Koop in early August 1986 and reached five major conclusions, which affirmed the findings of the Attorney General's Commission on Pornography.

10. *What were the findings?*

  a. That children used in pornography experience long-term adverse effects.

  b. Use of pornography causes one to believe that less common sexual practices really are common.

   c. Pornography that portrays sexual aggression as pleasurable increases the acceptance of coercion.

   d. Acceptance of coercion appears to be related to sexual aggression, and

   e. In laboratory settings, short term effects show exposure to violent pornography increases punishing behavior toward women. [23]

11. *Didn't some social scientists who testified before the commission claim their findings were misrepresented?*

Professors Donnerstein and Strauss were called by some reporters and given false information about the commission's findings based on their studies. The comments based on the false information were printed in the *New York Times*. [24] A month later, Donnerstein and Strauss participated in the Surgeon General's Workshop on Pornography and Public Health.

12. *Some experts have argued that there will never be conclusive proof that a causal connection exists between obscenity and violence toward women and children.*

The report acknowledges that most consequences are caused by numerous factors and, if *conclusive* means no other possibility exists, then social science proof never can be conclusive with any subject under consideration. Two of the largest categories of pornography consumers were not studied—the man who spends virtually all his spare time at the adult bookstore and the 12- to 17-year-old adolescent. If social scientists want to know the effects on adolescents, then they must expose adolescents to large amounts of pornography and see what happens. But this, of course, is not ethically possible.

13. *The 1970 Commission on Obscenity and Pornography found that pornography actually could be helpful to the consumer.*

The findings of that commission have been so discredited that the Senate refused to accept them. They were contradicted, not only by the Attorney General's Commission on Pornography in 1986, but by the Surgeon General's Workshop on Pornography and Public Health, which followed in August, as well as the 1969 report of the National Commission on the Causes and Prevention of Crime and the 1972 Surgeon General's Report on Television Violence and Social Behavior. The Attorney General's Commission heard testimony from countless people who claimed pornography is good for our culture, but couldn't find one person who was willing to testify, even behind a screen, that pornography benefitted him or her.

14. *The 1970 Commission supported the safety value theory—that pornography provides an outlet for people with potentially dangerous sex urges. Hasn't pornography legalization worked in Denmark?*

Since 1970, pornographers have quoted a Danish study by Kutchinsky that alleged that the number of reported sex crimes dropped after pornography was legalized. In that study, Kutchinsky lumped voyeurism and homosexuality with rape. However, those activities also were legalized, so naturally the total number of sex crimes went down. [25]

15. *What about other countries that have legalized pornography?*

Cross-national data from areas as separate as England, Australia, Singapore and South Africa show that rape rates have increased where pornography laws have been liberalized.[26]

16. *What about the 1984 study done on pornography for the Canadian government? Weren't its finding similar to the 1970 Pornography Commission in the U.S.?*

Yes. That committee relied heavily on a report by H.B. McKay. The major influence on his work was done by feminist Thelma McCormack, who ignored the recognized authorities and experts who have studied sex offenders' use of pornography. Neither McCormack nor McKay has done research in that field.[27]

17. *Surely there is an argument for pornography in the area of education.*

Just because you show everything and do everything doesn't mean you teach anything useful. Pornography teaches hatred and violence toward women and children.

18. *There are those who argue that pornography is a victimless crime and therefore should not be prosecuted.*

Kiddie porn cannot be made without a victim. Feminist author Andrea Dworkin said in her testimony before the Attorney General's Commission on Pornography that 65 to 70 percent of the women in pornography were victims of incest or child sex. Victims frequently are runaways who are raped. The rapes are filmed and then the victim blackmailed into remaining in the profession.[28]

19. *Should indecency on cable TV be regulated?*

Yes, indecency is indecency wherever it is, in a book or magazine or videocassette or invading your home through cable TV. The Cable Communications Act of 1984 declared indecency on TV the joint responsibility of the FCC and the Justice Department. The American people have a responsibility to hold these two agencies accountable.

20. *What about pornography on cable TV?*

The 1934 Communications Act stated that the airwaves belong to the American people and are a national resource: therefore, radio and TV stations must act in the public interest. The federal criminal code has a penalty for "whoever utters any obscene, indecent or profane language by means of radio communication." The Supreme Court extended this to television in *FCC v. Pacifica* in 1978.

What we have today, in terms of pornography, was unthinkable in 1934. The criminal code for broadcasters should be rewritten to include obscene, indecent or profane acts, as well as words. Clearly the intent was to make the standards higher for the airwaves that invade the privacy of our homes than for the local newsstands. Cable systems that transmit by closed circuit wires have the same access to our homes.

21. *Yes, but you don't have to subscribe.*

Many people live in areas where cable is the only way to receive decent television reception of any kind. Others live in areas where little is offered on the local channels.

Many people want and enjoy networks like CBN, TBN, CNN and C-SPAN. They have the right to receive them without being exposed to indecency.

22. *You can always change the channel and you can order a lock box to protect your children.*

Channels often bleed over, and children are curious. I can put potentially dangerous cleaners and chemicals out of their reach, but this is impossible with the TV set. There is no lock box that can match a child's curiosity. Porn also is available on many public access channels. Cable and satellite TV invade our homes. It is not my responsibility to turn the dial, it is the cable operator's responsibility not to bring it into my home. Saying that you can turn the dial is like saying you can run away from a mugger after you have been assaulted.

23. *Should Dial-a-Porn be illegal?*

Technically, it is illegal for children under 18, but of course this is totally unenforceable. It should be illegal, period—because it invades your home and it offers easy access to children.

24. *What about pornography in rock music? Is this a problem?*

The National Association of Broadcasters, the National Education Association and the Parent Teachers Association all agree that this is a serious problem. Many of the songs aimed at our young people contain sexually explicit language and strong messages about drugs, suicide and violence. Some attempt is being made to keep these songs from being played on radio and TV, but songs with these messages are often included in albums with a popular, more acceptable song.

25. *Aren't record companies labeling albums or printing lyrics on album covers now?*

Yes, but at present this is voluntary and not enforceable.

26. *Are the messages on records really harmful to children?*

Often repeated phrases have been found to change behavior. Why do companies spend money on radio commercials or clever jingles in TV advertising? They produce results. The late Jimi Hendrix said, "You can hypnotize people with music and when they get at their weakest point, you can preach into their subconscious minds what you want to say."[29]

27. *Is there any connection between these lyrics and teenage suicide?*

"The National Education Association estimates that many of the 5,000 teenage suicides each year are linked to depression fueled by fatalistic music and lyrics."[30]

28. *Isn't the size of the pornography industry alone a clear indication that people want it?*

Polls show that only 4 to 6 percent of the American people feel there should be no restrictions on pornography, and 76 percent want sexually violent movies and magazines banned altogether.[31] Also, 75 percent of the people in the U.S. agree there should be a rating system on records so that people are aware of the contents before they buy.[32]

29. *If you don't like pornographic films, books, records and videos, you don't have to see or hear them, but is it right to interfere with someone else's rights?*

You have the right to soft-core pornography, but not to obscenity. As an American citizen, I have a right to be protected from obscenity and the effects of obscenity, just as I have the right to be protected from street crime and drunk drivers. In defining obscenity, the Supreme Court says it must be judged by community standards, so if what you like isn't available in your community, then you also have the right to move to another community. If you move to a community where the majority want to consume this type of material, it most likely will be available. That's democracy at work.

7

WHAT ABOUT SEX EDUCATION AND SCHOOL-BASED HEALTH CLINICS?

More than a million teens become pregnant each year and almost half that number have abortions.[1]

Over 29,000 Americans have contracted AIDS, more than 16,000 have died. The Centers for Disease Control in Atlanta estimates that 1.5 million Americans now carry the virus but display no symptoms, and 179,000 are predicted to die by 1991.[2]

Teen pregnancy and abortion are serious problems; AIDS is a national emergency. All are symptoms of one common disease—immorality.

SYMPTOMS OF A DEADLY DISEASE

What is immorality? The dictionary defines it as wickedness; wrongdoing; lack of chastity. Immorality can strike anyone. It is not a respecter of race, creed or heritage. Its victims are found in all economic, social and intellectual levels. It is not confined to atheists. The disease of immorality is a deadly killer.

Do you not know that the wicked will not inherit
the kingdom of God? Do not be deceived: Neither the sexually immoral nor idolaters nor
adulterers nor male prostitutes nor homosexual
offenders nor thieves nor the greedy nor drunk-
ards nor slanderers nor swindlers will inherit
the kingdom of God (1 Cor. 6:9).

Planned Parenthood president, Faye Wattleton, says
the answer to teenage pregnancy is "not in preaching the
return to the morality of an earlier time, but in making certain teens have ready access to both sex education and
contraceptives."[3]

Those in the family planning and population control
business are working together to combine their brand of
comprehensive sex education with school-based health
clinics, which will dispense birth control pills, condoms and
other devices from offices inside our junior and senior high
schools to children aged 11-18, and refer them for abortions without their parents' knowledge or consent.[4]

VALUE-FREE SEX EDUCATION

What happened to that morality of an earlier time?
What really started the sexual revolution of the '60s? Was
it the secular humanists, the media, rock 'n' roll, the pill?

In 1961, there was a Conference on Church and Family
called by the National Council of Churches. Representatives from 28 Protestant churches met with various educators and scientists to discuss sex and marriage. This delegation asserted that "sex codes requiring too high a level
of ethical sensitivity are harmful," and called for "under-

standing, tolerance and reform" as a meaningful Christian ethic of sexual behavior.[5]

As a result of this, the Sex Information and Education Council of the U.S. (SIECUS) was born. SIECUS works right along with Planned Parenthood to provide value-free sex education programs for public schools.

Where were the Bibles during that conference?

> See to it that no one takes you captive through hollow and deceptive philosophy, which depends on human tradition and the basic principles of this world rather than on Christ (Col. 2:8).

On the surface, value-free sex education sounds like a reasonable solution. Is it really fair to expect the world to maintain Judeo-Christian standards?

One of the books widely used to impart value-free sex education by the public schools, school-based health clinics and those organizations that call themselves family planners, is *Changing Bodies, Changing Lives* by Ruth Bell and several other authors, including Tim Wernette, who was Planned Parenthood's director of education in Los Angeles. The book states: The only time any sex is perverted or immoral is if it is being forced on someone, or someone is doing it under pressure";[6] and "People aren't born knowing how to be in a sexual relationship, so you have to learn a lot with each partner."[7]

This book goes on to explain various kinds of sexual activity, including anal and oral sex. It tells its young readers that they may begin to notice that they are attracted to someone of their own sex. "For some, that self-awareness and understanding is a natural and positive thing."[8] It goes on to describe how gay people *come out* and meet each other. It says that lesbians sometimes meet through "shared political work in the women's movement."[9] It describes the *cruising* activities of gay men and goes into the details of how to make eye contact with a stranger and so on.[10]

It offers a lot of advice in dealing with parents. If they don't want you to be sexual at all until some distant time, you may feel you have to tune out their voice entirely."[11]

In an earlier book called *Our Bodies, Ourselves,* Ruth Bell used an illustration of a sexual fantasy with animals in the same nonjudgmental way.[12] Is this *value-free?* No! Just as there is no such thing as a law that is morally neutral, morally neutral sex education is nonexistent. Moral standards can be set high or low. We simply have settled for the lowest common denominator.

What does the Bible have to say to us about these matters?

> Do not lie with a man as one lies with a woman; that is detestable. Do not have sexual relations with an animal and defile yourself with it. A woman must not present herself to an animal to have sexual relations with it; that is a perversion (Lev. 18:22,23).
>
> Because of this, God gave them over to shameful lusts. Even their women exchanged natural relations for unnatural ones. In the same way the men also abandoned natural relations with women and were inflamed with lust for one another. Men committed indecent acts with other men, and received in themselves the due penalty for their perversion (Rom. 1:26,27).

Don't you know that you yourselves are God's temple and that God's Spirit lives in you? If anyone destroys God's temple, God will destroy him; for God's temple is sacred, and you are that temple (1 Cor. 3:16,17).

See also Genesis 2:24; Exodus 20:14; Proverbs 7:1,5,26,27; Matthew 5:27-29.

THE COST OF IMMORALITY

What is the cost of immorality in U.S. dollars? For AIDS, the federal spending has jumped to $411,000,000 each year for research and education.[13] Estimates of medical costs are up to $150,000 for every AIDS patient.[14]

Teen sex has become big business here in this country; $442 million was spent to help fund family planning clinics and extend contraceptive services to our youth by federal, state and local governments in 1981, up from $11 million in 1971.[15] Has it helped?

Researchers Stan Weed and Joseph A. Olsen studied the effects of this dramatic increase in spending on teenage pregnancy and abortion rates. They discovered that for every 1,000 teens enrolled in these clinics, 50 to 120 *more* pregnancies occurred.[16]

Dr. Jacqueline R. Kasun, professor of Economics at Humboldt State University, just completed a state-by-state study and reached a similar conclusion: states that spend the most on contraceptives and abortions tend to have the highest rate of teenage abortions plus unmarried births. California, the leading spender in this category—$95 million—has a teen pregnancy rate 30 percent above the national level. By contrast, states which reduced spending on these services or required parental consent for minors to obtain birth control or abortions, saw their teen pregnancy rates drop dramatically. [17]

At present, there are 76 school-based health clinics dispensing birth control pills and other contraceptives from inside the public schools to children as young as 12[18], and about 5,000 community family planning clinics around the country that distribute contraceptives to teenagers. [19]

Secretary of Education William Bennett strongly disagrees with this approach. He says schools should stress abstinence and should teach about sex only as part of marriage. Bennett argues that to dispense contraceptives in schools "is to throw up one's hands and say, 'We give up.'"[20] In a statement released jointly with Surgeon General C. Everett Koop, Bennett said, "Sex education that accepts children's sexual activity as inevitable and focuses only on 'safe sex' will be at best ineffectual, at worst itself a cause of serious harm."[21]

PLANS UNDERWAY

Despite the opposition from Bennett, the Center for Population Options favors putting school-based health clinics in every junior and senior high school in America, according to American Life League president, Judie Brown (*Focus on the Family,* October 1986, p. 2). Proposed legislation for studies and funding must be fought at the local, state and national level. To find out the status of school-based health clinics in your area and how you can help, contact a pro-family or pro-life organization today. The ideal time to approach your school board and your state legislators is *before* a study on adolescent pregnancy has been proposed.

The more teens are exposed to contraceptives, the higher the pregnancy rate among teens. The higher the pregnancy rate, the more abortions are performed. The more abortions that are performed, the more money collected by Planned Parenthood's own abortion clinics. "Nearly 30 percent of the 95,000 women who obtained abortions at Planned Parenthood centers last year were 19 or under."[22]

Faye Wattleton says, "We're never out of the business of defending the right to legal abortion."[23] What has been left unsaid in the wake of all these new studies? There is no abortion for AIDS!

The answer, according to all these family planners, is more comprehensive sex education, more school-based health clinics, more contraceptives for teens and above all—more money, please!

QUESTIONS AND ANSWERS

1. *What are school-based health clinics?*

Facilities designed to operate from inside our junior and senior high schools to provide birth control information, contraceptives and abortion referrals for our children. These clinics are developed and promoted by the Center for Population Options, Planned Parenthood and others in the business of providing family planning, abortion and abortion-related services.

2. *Isn't family planning just one of the many areas of health services available at a school-based health clinic?*

It is interesting that you refer to the practice of giving contraceptives to children as family planning. Many parents of these children scheduled to receive the free contraceptives and how-to advice are lured by the promise of free health care. The clinic usually is headed by a nurse with the same training as the traditional school nurse, but with some additional instruction in birth control. Armed with drawers of condoms, birth control pills and other contraceptive devices, the nurse, in reality, treats minor ailments and makes referrals. Local doctors who have been contracted to visit the clinics a few hours a week often do little more than set up appointments for abortions.

3. *Are all students free to use the clinics?*

Parents are asked to sign blanket consent forms. Once they do this, they will not know what happens inside the clinics unless the student requests the parent be told. This is no accident. The Center for Population Options claims this is necessary "to assure minors access to family planning information."[24] Unfortunately, even if parents don't sign the form, their children still can be given these services in some states. If parents are given the option of crossing off these services on the form before signing it, it's often a sham.

4. *Wouldn't most parents be in favor of the confidentiality maintained at the clinics if it caused their teens to be more responsible about sex?*

Perhaps some would, but most parents don't want these clinics passing out birth control devices, and a Louis Harris poll conducted by Planned Parenthood in the fall of 1986 showed that only 12 percent of our teenagers feel that contraceptives should be available in the schools.[25] In 1981, the state of Minnesota enacted a law requiring

parental notification for abortions and pregnancies. Teenage abortions and births decreased dramatically.[26]

5. *Who pays for these services?*

Ultimately, as taypayers, we all do. Initially, supporters
come in with funds from private foundations already heavily involved in population control. But all clinics must "look
to public support for continuation."[27] Estimates on what it
costs to run one of these clinics range from $25,000 to
$400,000 annually, depending on the number of children
served.[28]

6. *But aren't teenagers the most under-served medical seg-
ment of our society?*

That's because they are the healthiest segment of our
society. Most health services promised to be available in
the clinics are already available elsewhere in the community if they are needed. So it's a waste of money that could
be used for more classrooms, higher teacher salaries and
teaching our kids to read and write. The family planners
like to talk about the misconceptions children have about
sex. That's because so many of those kids in sex education
are functionally illiterate.

7. *Teenagers are going to have sex. That is a given, so isn't
it better to try to help them prevent pregnancies?*

According to a Louis Harris poll just completed for
Planned Parenthood, only 28 percent of teenagers have
had intercourse, ever. Michael Schwartz, of the Free Congress Research and Education Foundation, pointed out
flaws in over sampling certain groups. He reports that,

when adjusted, a more accurate figure would be 20 percent.[29] Also, many in this group have experienced sex and returned to abstinence, so, in spite of what we hear, *everybody is not doing it!*

8. *What about those who are going to do it anyway?*

There will always be those who will engage in unhealthy or immoral behavior, no matter how it is presented. Teen pregnancy has become big business. Abortion alone accounts for a half-billion dollars a year. Look at the number of people, directly involved in those clinics, who also are involved in the abortion business in some way. We set up giant bureaucracies to deal with this problem. Right now there are probably 15 bureaucrats for every pregnant teen. Are they really trying to solve this problem, or are they in the business of creating a multiplicity of services and creating jobs?

9. *Haven't classes in sex education, combined with school-based clinics, been proven effective in delaying sex and lowering pregnancy rates?*

No. A comprehensive study by Stan Weed and Joseph Olsen at the Institute for Research and Evaluation concluded that "for every 1,000 teens between 15 and 19 years of age enrolled in family planning clinics, we can expect between 50 to 120 *more* pregnancies."[30]

10. *Haven't you heard of the study done at Mechanic Arts High School in St. Paul where birthrates were cut nearly in half?*

There were similar clinics in two other St. Paul schools.

The St. Paul program has never published a scientifically valid study. Undocumented claims of decreased fertility rates have ranged from 23 to 66 percent. You should know, however, that the findings show a drop in the *birthrate,* not the *pregnancy rate;* the total female enrollment of the two schools during the period of the study dropped by almost 25 percent, and data was not compared to any other school with the same demographics but no clinic. Further, the Support Center for School-Based Clinics even acknowledged the data was based upon the clinic's own records and the staff's knowledge of births. "Thus the data undoubtedly do not include all births."[31]

11. *What about the study that showed the combination of sex education and school-based health clinics was effective in causing teenagers to delay sex?*

That study was done by Laurie Zabin on 1,033 teens in Baltimore, and printed in Planned Parenthood's magazine. It was refuted by Dr. Jacqueline Kasun, professor of Economics at Humboldt State University. The conclusions of the study were based on a decline of sexual activity in only 96 of the 1,033 girls surveyed at the beginning of the study. There were three times as many dropouts from the survey in the school with the clinic program as in the control school, and many of those dropouts may have been for reasons of pregnancy.[32]

12. *Shouldn't something be done about the 1.1 million teenage pregnancies every year?*

Definitely, but the first thing that should be done is to correct that figure given out by the family planners. Most of those teenagers were over 18 and out of high school.

Many were married.[33] The second thing we must realize is that pregnancy is just a symptom. We must treat the disease.

13. *What about the half-million or so teens who are getting pregnant each year?*

Exposure to contraceptives only increases this problem. Planned Parenthood stated in its own journal, "More teenagers are using contraceptives and using them more consistently than ever before. Yet the number and rate of premarital pregnancies continue to rise."[34]

14. *Why is this true?*

Parents can figure this out for themselves. Teenagers forget lunches, books, homework assignments and cleaning their rooms. How can we expect them to remember to use contraceptives consistently?

15. *Wouldn't the answer be to do a better job of teaching them about contraceptives in sex education classes?*

We're talking about children 11 years old and up. This is junior high and high school. When we tell children, "Only you can decide when it's right to become sexually active," then teach them how to have sex and hand them the contraceptives, we're placing too much responsibility on these children. This is child abuse—perhaps in its cruelest form.

16. *Why are you against sex education in the schools?*

I am not against sex education. I am against the kind of sex education that has been provided to our schools by

Planned Parenthood and similar groups, with no guidelines, no sense of right and wrong. There are two excellent sex education programs available. "Sex Respect," out of Golf, Illinois, developed by Colleen Kelly Mast, already has been approved by many states; and "Teen Aid," out of Spokane, Washington, has been available since 1981. Both promote abstinence until marriage, based on the principles of science, health and personal integrity.

17. *What's wrong with a program that simply educates and is value-neutral in that it does not encourage or discourage teen sexual activity?*

Sex education can't be value-neutral or objective. It is either presented as having moral parameters or as having no parameters, and even if you present it as having no parameters, you're still using someone's values.

18. *Isn't it true that no study ever has borne out that sex education has an effect on students' rate of sexual activity?*

The Planned Parenthood poll, conducted by Louis Harris, was most revealing. Its results indicate hardly any difference in the rate of sexual activity between those who had no sex education in school and those who had a course that was not considered *comprehensive* by Planned Parenthood. Sex education classes considered comprehensive by Planned Parenthood include the promotion of contraceptives. The rate of sexual activity among those who did have a comprehensive course was more than one-third higher than among the other two groups.[35]

19. *But isn't it true that Planned Parenthood teaches it is okay to say no to sex?*

When you say to teenagers that it's okay to say *no* to sex, are you not implying that most people are saying *yes?* This certainly doesn't help an adolescent make a responsible choice. That's a lot different from saying they *should* say *no* to sex until they are ready to establish a mutually faithful, monogamous relationship.

20. *But don't you agree that it's not the teachers' nor the schools' responsibility to set moral values?*

Schools don't seem to have any qualms about taking a *neutral* approach to morals when discussing lying, drugs, stealing or cheating on exams, so, in essence, they are already setting moral values.

21. *But these things are obviously harmful.*

So is sex when it is practiced by children. It causes disease, unwanted pregnancy, rejection, emotional distress and, in some cases, death. In addition to AIDS, there are more than 50 different sexually transmitted diseases.[36] Women who have had multiple sexual partners and/or intercourse at an early age are at greatest risk for cervical cancer;[37] and a 15-year-old sexually active girl has a one-in-eight chance of acquiring acute pelvic inflammatory disease, a condition that can leave her sterile, compared with a 1-in-80 risk for a sexually active 24-year-old woman.[38]

22. *You mention death. The AIDS epidemic is out of control. Isn't that reason enough to teach teens about safe sex?*

The only safe sex is abstinence until marriage. The failure

rate in condoms, if used *perfectly* under laboratory conditions, is 3 percent; in general use, it's up to 33 percent.[39] That means you can get pregnant one-third of the time, or catch AIDS one-third of the time. That's not good enough. That's sexual roulette. Until now, the big back-up for the failures created by the Planned Parenthood programs has been abortion. There is no abortion for AIDS.

8
NOW WHAT CAN I DO?

"Everybody talks about the weather but nobody does anything about it."[1]

Have you ever noticed that here in this country we spend almost as much time talking—or, more accurately, complaining—about the government as we do about those erratic atmospheric conditions that surround us? Think about it. Hardly a day goes by that you don't hear someone complaining about the government. If you pay close attention, the complaint you hear today might come from your very own lips. Unlike the weather, however, we can do something about the government besides complain.

KNOW YOUR ELECTED REPRESENTATIVES

Let me ask you an extremely personal question. Do you know the name of your congressional representative? When we talk about our national government, that's as personal as we can get. Your representative is your closest link to Washington. If you want a law passed or want to make sure your concern is accurately represented on Capitol Hill, your representative is your best bet.

If you can name your representative, give yourself a pat on the back. You deserve it. And the next time you hear someone complain about the government, get personal and ask them to name their congressional representative. You may be surprised. Most people can name the president and vice-president. Many folks can come up with the names of their two state senators, but only a few will know the name of the person most important to them when it comes to having their views expressed in the nation's capital.

Now let's get even more personal. Can you name your most important representative? By this, I mean the one representing the smallest area or fewest number of voters, the one whose attention you're most likely to get immediately in your state, in your county, in your city or town. Can you name him/her?

If you can, you're quite exceptional. Most people can't, but don't let this get you down. Because so few people even go to the trouble to find out the names of their most important elected representatives, when you do take the time to write, call or visit one of yours, you'll be pleased to find out just how important you are to them. They will value what you have to say *if* you've done your homework and *if* you say it in the right spirit.

FINDING THE KEY PEOPLE

Who are all these people? How are you going to find them, much less keep tabs on what they're doing? It may seem like an overwhelming task, but let me assure you, it isn't. It's not nearly as difficult as keeping track of your

The Key 16
U.S. Government Five

President	1600 Pennsylvania Avenue Washington, D.C. 20500
Vice President	Executive Office Bldg. Washington, D.C. 20501
Senator	
Senator	
Congressional Representative	

State Government Five

Governor	
Lt. Governor	
Attorney General	
State Senator	
Assemblyman	

Local Government Six

Mayor	
City Councilman	
School Board Member	
County Supervisor	
District Attorney	
Sheriff	

favorite football or baseball team. There are no college drafts, reentry drafts, supplemental drafts, farm systems, free agents, trades, holdouts, strikes, drug tests, disabled lists, injured reserve lists or even laundry lists. There are no players to be named later. You can't jump teams, cities or leagues. You pick these folks and send them where you want them and they stay there—as long as you're happy with what they're doing. When you're not, you simply get a few of your friends—sometimes a lot of friends—together and elect others to take their places.

Compared to memorizing team rosters, learning your elected representatives is a piece of cake. There are only 16 key people and unless you've just arrived from Outer Mongolia, you already know at least four of them. Take a couple of minutes right now, look over the chart and see how many names you can fill in. Six is about average, nine is pretty good, and anything above 12 is exceptional. The space at the right is for their addresses and phone numbers. Notice spaces for your two U.S. senators, congressional representative, state senator and assemblyman. These elected officials maintain two offices. The exception would be for your state representatives if you live in the city that happens to be your state's capital.

While you're obtaining the addresses and phone numbers, don't be tempted to record the information for only one office. Although most elected representatives check with their local office daily, there will be times when you may want to get your message to him or her immediately. If you're planning a visit to your state's capital or the nation's capital, you can usually schedule a personal visit with one of your representatives, if you do it far enough in advance. So it's good to have information on both offices available.

A word about the space marked *Assemblyman.* That space is for your representative to the lower house of your state's legislature. Every state except Nebraska has a two-house (bicameral) legislature patterned after our national legislative branch. Every upper house is called the *senate,* and most lower houses, the *house of representatives,* but four states use the term *assembly,* and three, the *house of delegates.* The combined houses are called the general assembly or the legislative assembly, except in Massachusetts and New Hampshire. Those two states call their legislatures the *general court.*

Where to Find Them

But how do you find which representatives at the national, state and local levels are yours? You can begin by looking in the front of the white pages of most phone books. The government listings are somewhere between the telephone company information and the regular listings. City government is usually first.

Look under the appropriate headings. Under city government you'll find listings for the mayor's office, city attorney and so on, right along with the fire department, library, and building and zoning. You'll find locating your city councilman and school board member a little more of a challenge this way. These are usually listed by district and, in a large city, how do you know which district is yours?

The simple thing is to turn to your county listings and look for the register of voters. You probably will find a number for general information and in that office you'll usually find a full-time employee whose only job is to find your elected representatives for you on all levels. Just give this person your address and you'll have all the information you need for your key government officials in just minutes.

The last officeholder on your list is the sheriff. This person usually is an elected official, and is sometimes confused with the chief of police, who usually is appointed. If you live in the city, the police department takes care of law enforcement, but the county is usually in the hands of the sheriff's department. In an emergency, the sheriff's department will step in to assist the city. For this reason, city dwellers usually participate in the election of the sheriff.

When I've used the word *usually* it's because, here in the United States, counties and towns are free to establish their local governments any way the people who live in them choose. The information on exactly how yours is established should be available from the person in the registrar's office.

When you get the information on how your local government is set up, you may want to add one or two officials to your chart, or even delete one. It would be impossible for me to give you a list that would apply to everyone. You may have a key 15 or 17.

I want to encourage you not just to put the information on your elected representatives in this book. After you've finished reading it, you might loan the book to a friend, accidentally leave it somewhere, or put it away on a shelf.

Before you go any further, create at least a page for your key representatives in your address book. Don't file each one alphabetically. If you do that before they've fully become a part of your life, you'll forget their names, never find them again and be back where you started. My address book has subject headings instead of the alphabetical listings, so it's easy. I have a separate page for city, county and country. You can create a page, or pages, under *R* for representatives or *G* for government. If your address book isn't expandable, you can write or type the information on another page and staple or tape it into the appropriate place.

All of this may seem like a lot of trouble. Right now you may feel like you need this information only at home where you can sit down to write a letter or make a phone call. But let me warn you, if you wait for the time to do it at home, you may never find the time to get it done. You may want to write some post cards on the bus, make that phone call between appointments or give information to a friend over lunch. If you have it with you, you'll find ways to use it.

More importantly, 1 Timothy 2:1-2 urges that "prayers, intercession and thanksgiving be made for . . . all those in authority, that we may live peaceful and quiet lives in all godliness and holiness." That page of representatives' names just may become the most significant part of your prayer list. Pray for your elected representatives by name daily.

Get Organized

Now that you know just who your representatives are, the next step is to find out what they are doing on your behalf. I'll have to admit, this part is a little more difficult. Remember when you started this book I asked you to pick out just one issue and work your way up? You may still be on number one or you may have two or three by now. Begin by keeping track of your issue or issues. It's really a lot like keeping up with your favorite team. You scan the sports section, and the Miami Dolphins, New York Rangers, Chicago Cubs or Los Angeles Lakers—depending on your favorite or favorites—just pop right out.

Make a commitment today to scan just one newspaper. It's a good idea to make it a local newspaper. In large papers, the first section usually contains all the national news. The local news has its own special section farther back. This is for what's happening right now. There may be a feature story pertaining to your issue(s) almost anywhere. Most papers have a little block somewhere on page one or two that will give you highlights of the major stories covered that day and where to find them. Be sure to scan the editorial page as well, but don't spend too much time with any one part. Better to miss a few stories than have it take so much of your time every day that you get discouraged and quit.

Put a couple of highlighter pens and scissors in your office desk or around the house, wherever you are most likely to read the paper. If it is at home, have an understanding with your family that, if they are borrowed, they are to be promptly returned—kids love to use the highlighter pens to color things.

When you're scanning the paper, highlight as you go so you won't have to search for the information again. No big deal if you highlight something and, by the time you get to the end of the article or down a few lines, you find you didn't want it after all. It's a lot quicker than going back after you've read the article. Work for *light speed*. We're talking quantity, not quality here. You will probably find two or three stories you'll want to cut out and save for reference. Indicate on each clipping when and where you got it.

Remember, you need factual, current information so you are ready to speak out when the opportunity comes, and when you're ready, it *will* come. "So he reasoned in the synagogue with the Jews and the God-fearing Greeks, as well as in the marketplace day by day with those who happened to be there" (Acts 17:17).

INFORMATION AT YOUR FINGERTIPS

Now, where will you put these articles? If you work in an office, you have file drawers already, and it will be easy to slip in a new file as you take on another issue. If you work in another environment or at home and haven't discovered file drawers, let me encourage you to invest in a file cabinet. You'll be amazed at some of the things you can file away and reclaim when you need them, such as income tax information, the dog's rabies certificate, your child's artwork—you get the idea.

If you're not completely sold on a file cabinet or don't want to invest a lot of money, try some cardboard file drawers or large plastic file boxes; those big enough to file 8½″ × 11″ pages, not the index card size. You can buy these one by one and put them almost anywhere.

Another way to keep this information is to buy a looseleaf notebook with the rings that open and close. You may want a separate notebook for each issue or you can use tabs to separate them. Use a hole punch for page-size items. You can use cellophane tape or staples to attach other information to notebook paper. Want to share the information at a meeting? Just pick up your file folder or notebook and off you go on a moment's notice.

HOW TO AVOID OVERWHELM

When we turn on the TV or radio, we are constantly bombarded by news, most of it bad. Some stations give you news 24 hours a day. Even the major network stations offer four to five hours of news each day. There is no way you can watch it all. It's enough to make even the most thoughtful, together person feel downright uninformed. It's no wonder we often retreat to music, movies or situation comedies and ignore the news altogether.

We have a radio station in my city—KFWB, Los Angeles—that says, "If you give us 22 minutes, we'll give you the world." It's basically just headlines, most stories lasting around 30 seconds, skipping from one subject to another. Believe it or not, in 22 minutes you can get a pretty good grip on what's going on in your town and the world. A lot of days, that's all I have, so I tune in while I'm getting dressed, driving to my aerobics class or putting on my make-up. If I hear a news story concerning an issue that's important to me, I turn to another station for a more expanded story or make a point to catch it on the nightly news. If I've found out all I feel I need to know at that hour, I dial in "Focus on the Family" or some good music and relax.

Radio is wonderful; you can take it with you wherever you go. Some little ones you can wear like a tiny pair of earmuffs. You can wear them bicycling, jogging, doing the laundry, grocery shopping or mowing the lawn. There is only one valid reason for not being informed today—you don't care.

As for nightly TV newscasts, most are excellent, but don't beat yourself up mentally if you can't work them into your schedule. If you do watch, it's a good idea not to get stuck on one station or network. Train yourself to alternate so that you get different viewpoints.

My most-watched TV is in the kitchen. The news is always on at the dinner hour and I can glance at it while I'm cooking (gives me an excuse for burning the vegetables).

I don't like to watch TV while eating. That's an important family time, but we often finish dinner before the network news. Then we sit down for 30 minutes to watch it together. It's especially helpful to do this with your school age children. You'll be surprised at the dividends this will pay in their schoolwork!

If you're near a TV in the morning you can watch the "Today" show or "Good Morning America." It's a lot more fun than watching the evening news, and some people feel, even more helpful.

I also want to encourage you to subscribe to one of the weekly newsmagazines, scanning it the same way you do the newspapers, with pens and scissors in hand. Experiment before you subscribe to a magazine. Buy one this week, another next week, and keep alternating for awhile. You'll find the editors have different viewpoints, and some will give more space and balance to your issues.

Now these weekly magazines are expensive. You may want to share the cost of a subscription with a friend. Read it with your highlighter, then pass it along. Your friend, in turn, reads it with the highlighter and is responsible for clipping the highlighted articles and making photocopies for you. Next month, it's your turn to be last.

Another wonderful alternative, if you live or work near a library, is to spend your lunch hour there once a week, or an hour while waiting for the kids at Little League or music lessons. You can really work on your *light-speed* scanning technique and photocopy the articles you want to take with you when you leave. Again, note on each one the name of publication, date and page number. Remember, the important thing is not how many of those magazines you can get through, but that you are being consistent.

Selecting and Joining an Organization

Keeping up with the issues takes commitment and per-
severance. You'll soon find that the more you *network*
(work with others), the easier it will become.

I mentioned earlier that you might share a magazine
subscription with a friend. Better still, if you're a member
of a Bible study, prayer or support group, ask each member to scan a different news magazine or newspaper each
week for the significant articles on the issues your group
feels are important.

One of the easiest and most effective ways to monitor
your issues is to join an organization. There is an organization for every issue we've covered here. Some deal with
all or several of the issues in this book, others with only
one. These organizations publish newsletters and magazines that will keep you updated on all the material affect-
ing their issues, including legislation before Congress and
the various state legislatures. They let you know which
bills are coming up for a vote, and many give you regular
reports to let you know how your representatives are voting.

Joining an organization really gives you and/or your
small group an opportunity to expand your horizons as well
as your network. It also gives you a big voice instantly on
Capitol Hill. A representative of an organization of several
hundred thousand citizens concerned about a particular
issue will get immediate attention.

Membership prices in these organizations vary. All are
low, however, and most rely heavily on donations to keep
going. The individuals who run and work for these organizations are a special breed. They are extremely dedicated,
and usually overworked and underpaid. They depend on

us, not only for support, but for encouragement as well. Remember, they need us and we need them.

You will find a list of some of these organizations in the appendix of this book. They are just a few of the organizations that are ready, willing and, most likely, able to help you. Pick out one or two that interest you, and then write for information and a sample copy of their newsletter or magazine. If you have a specific question on an issue and you don't know where to find the answer, write to one of these groups and ask them if they can help you or direct you to one that can.

You're not in this battle by yourself, although when you first begin to look around your neighborhood or your church, it may seem that way for awhile. Remember the words of the reformer Wendell Phillips: "One on God's side is a majority."[2] If you don't have a group that shares your views, ask God for one and be open to the people and the opportunities He puts in your path.

What can you do today? Join an organization; attend that first meeting; call the local office of your congressman to express your opinion on a bill coming up for a vote; answer a child's question about one of the issues; write a letter to a television network or sponsor, to the editor of a newspaper, to your mother; speak to your Sunday School class.

Remember, God works through people. Mary Crowley, the dynamic woman who built Home Interiors and Gifts into a multimillion-dollar enterprise, made this powerful statement of two-letter words: "If it is to be, it is up to me."[3]

Go for it!

9
CAN ONE PERSON REALLY MAKE A DIFFERENCE?

"Ask not what your country can do for you—ask what you can do for your country."[1]

Those familiar words, uttered by the youngest man ever elected president of the United States, are perhaps even more relevant today than they were back in 1961 when John Fitzgerald Kennedy delivered them in his inaugural address.

What can you do for our country? At the very least you can be an informed, registered voter. Maybe that doesn't sound like much to you alongside the accomplishments of a man like John F. Kennedy, but consider the fact that Kennedy won that election back in 1960 with a margin of just one-half vote per precinct.[2] A handful of voters controlled the fate of this president and gave him the opportunity to do something for his country from the highest office in the land.

How important is one vote? Literally a handful of voters have controlled this country time and time again.

ONE VOTE CAN MAKE A DIFFERENCE

One vote was important to Kennedy, but one vote was even more important to Lyndon Baines Johnson, the man who succeeded Kennedy when he was assassinated on November 22, 1963. If just 87 people in Texas had stayed home and had not cast their one vote for Johnson in his race for the Senate against Coke Stevenson in 1948, chances are he would have been stopped on his road to the presidency. That was Johnson's margin of victory. He was given the nickname "Landslide Lyndon" at that time, and that nickname stayed with him until he died in 1973. Lyndon Johnson never forgot the importance of one vote. [3]

An even closer senatorial election occurred in the state of Nevada in 1964. Howard Cannon retained his seat that year by only 48 votes. [4]

Grover Cleveland was elected president in 1884 by just a handful of folks in New York. Oh, the other states voted, all right, but just 575 voters in his home state gave him the margin he needed in the electoral college to become our twenty-second president. [5]

As late as 1976, a few people in just two states could have changed the course of our nation's history. If one person in each precinct in Ohio and six in each precinct in Mississippi had voted for Gerald Ford, Jimmy Carter would not have been our thirty-ninth president. [6]

The examples of close-call elections on the state and local level are too numerous to mention, but one of the most dramatic occurred in the state of Massachusetts many years ago. Marcus Morton needed a majority of 51,034 votes to become governor, and that's exactly what he received. [7]

In 1984, in Waterbury, Connecticut, Joan Hartley won

her state legislative race by only two votes out of nearly 10,000 cast.[8]

What about congressional races? Remember your congressman is your most important link to Capitol Hill.

In 1984, six house seats in North Carolina were decided by 2 percent or less of the eligible voters.[9]

In 1984, Frank McCloskey was finally declared the winner by four votes in Indiana's eighth Congressional District over Richard McIntyre after several recounts.[10] That same year, Joe Barton made it to the House of Representatives after winning a primary runoff in Texas by only 10 votes.[11]

Just think of it—10 votes—that's your vote and nine friends. Do you know 10 people in your state who didn't vote in the last election for one reason or another? I'll bet you do.

Only 64.1 percent of all those eligible to vote in this country are even registered. That means over 62 million people have never even bothered to exercise one of their most precious freedoms, a freedom many of our ancestors fought and died for.[12] The sad fact is that only about half of Americans of voting age go to the polls on election day[13] and the percentage of Christian voters is even less.[14]

Why?

The act of casting a ballot is the easy part. It only takes a few minutes of your time. Automation and the number of polling places have virtually cut out the long lines—but casting an *informed* ballot is another matter.

The sheer number of offices and issues is often mind-boggling, even in a local election. So many people wait until the last minute to look them over, and then quietly retreat, victims of *overwhelm*. How can you avoid overwhelm?

If you'll apply my scanning and clipping technique (described in chapter eight) for updating your issues before the next election, voting will be a snap. Remember, if you're not familiar with a candidate or an issue, you can skip that part. It's not necessary to vote for every office or measure to have your ballot counted.

Why not try teamwork for your next election? Divide the offices and issues among your prayer group, Bible study or Sunday School class. Pick a date a week or two before the election. Have everyone bring their sample ballots and share information.

What can you do for your country? It may not seem like a big thing, but why not begin by making your one vote count in the next election?

"Most people would succeed in small things if they were not troubled with great ambitions."[15]

How to Make Your Vote Equal 100

Have you ever been so mad at how one of your elected officials voted on a piece of legislation that you wanted to tell that official a thing or two but . . . you didn't?

Have you ever wanted to thank an elected representative for *hanging tough* on an issue but . . . you didn't?

Have you ever felt so strongly about a pending piece of legislation that you wanted your representatives to know just how you felt before they voted on it but . . . you didn't let them know?

Have you ever had some relevant information on an issue before Congress or your state legislature that you hoped your representative had but . . . you didn't share it?

Have you ever seen an injustice done to someone or been a victim of an injustice yourself that you knew a new bill or law would correct but . . . you didn't let anyone with

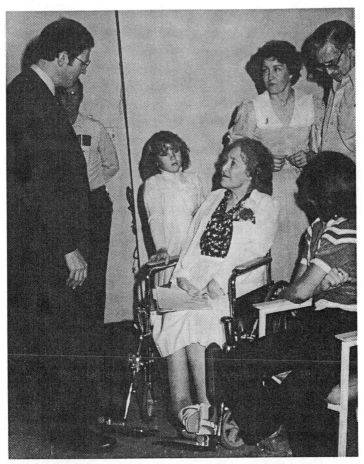

Senator William L. Armstrong meets with Mrs. May
Reser, the persistent lady he credits with influencing the
passage of the Social Security Disability Benefits
Amendment through her letters and phone calls to his
office.

the authority to introduce that bill or law know about it?

If you answered yes to any or all of the above, welcome to the majority! So few people ever write to one of their elected officials that most legislators count each letter they do receive as representing the sentiments of 100 voters. They feel that for everyone who actually took the time to put pen to paper, 100 people feel the same way about the issue and meant to write, but didn't.

Less than 20 percent of the population has ever written to one of their elected representatives.[16] When you take the time to do it, you might say your one letter equals 100 letters. It's the easiest way I know to multiply your vote.

Richard Cizik, in his book, *The High Cost of Indifference,* quoted one veteran government official on the subject of letter writing: "If the average member of Congress received as many as half a dozen letters scrawled in pencil on brown wrapping paper, it would be enough to change his vote on most issues."[17]

Perhaps he did exaggerate just a bit, but the question remains, if letters are so very important and can really make a difference, why don't more people write them?

I feel there are two reasons, and I'll just bet you are way ahead of me about now and have already jumped to reason number one—*time!*

May Reser, of Westminster, Colorado, never seemed to have the time to write to one of her congressional representatives. Oh, on many occasions in her 56 years she'd wanted to do it, but she never did. Now, May had time problems most of us never have to experience. Just getting out of bed in the morning was a task in itself. You see, May Reser is a quadriplegic and, when she writes, she does it with a mouth stick.

In 1982, all disability recipients were under review by the Social Security Administration. The review was legislated in 1979 during the Carter administration, and the process had turned into a nightmare for many disabled people during the three years that followed. Many were indiscriminately being tossed off the roles. May was not on disability, but her husband was, and she was aware of many injustices. She knew of people who were hurting so badly they had contemplated suicide. They had no money for food and basic help while their cases were on appeal.

May didn't have much hope when she wrote a letter, detailing the injustices, to one of her senators, Bill Armstrong, who was chairman of the Senate Social Security subcommittee. However, she felt she had to do it anyway. She followed up her letter with a phone call which led to a meeting with Howard Propst, the senator's top aide. Propst was deeply touched and impressed by May's presentation. She not only detailed the problems, but she offered good suggestions to help the Social Security Administration solve those problems.

After hearing Propst's report, Senator Armstrong rolled up his sleeves and went to work. Legislation had already been introduced to restore benefits to the disabled while their eligibility was being reviewed. Inspired by May Reser, Senator Armstrong worked with others and got this legislation enacted in the waning moments of the Ninety-eighth Congress. The Social Security Disability Benefits Amendment was passed, and Armstrong gave all the credit to May Reser.

President Reagan wrote a letter commending Mrs. Reser for her work. Senator Armstrong had it framed for her, along with one of the pens used to sign the bill into law. Today, a lot of disabled people are well and happy because May Reser made the time to write that letter.

HELP! I'M DROWNING IN PAPERWORK!

It's amazing how much paperwork is handled in the average home these days. Sometimes I feel as if I'm in a lifeboat bobbing up and down on a sea of the stuff. It's not just the household bills anymore; there are actually companies out there created just to buy and sell mailing lists containing your name and address and mine. Have you ever noticed that, when you buy something from one store, you suddenly get about 438 new catalogs from stores and mail-order houses you have never heard of? Even if you don't order anything or join anything, they create mailing lists by zip codes.

Every child adds his own wave of paperwork to your sea: consent forms, report cards, Sunday School forms, carpool sign-ups, progress reports, health forms, camp information, class objectives, school schedules. Every new activity adds to the height of that particular wave: scouts, gymnastics, swimming, Little League, soccer—need I say more? It's no wonder we are often swamped!

Now I readily admit that paperwork has been my undoing; it's my Achilles' heel. At times I let it pile up so high, I've had to stay up all night before a trip just to handle all the things that couldn't possibly wait until I got back. It finally got so bad I had to admit I was a *paperholic* and I joined *Paperwork Anonymous (PA)*.

Before PA, there were times I couldn't find my desk. Sometimes I couldn't find my office. And when I did, it was dangerous to open the door because the sea of paperwork came tumbling out to greet me. Adding a much-needed letter to my congressman to that sea would have been all that was needed to sink my lifeboat for sure! I couldn't bear to think of it. Well, okay, not for very long anyway.

So far as I know, I'm the only member of PA, but I invite you to become one. Here are the rules:

1. Assess your own personal sea and establish a realistic timetable to clear it out. Even if it's a paper ocean, allow no more than six days for this task. Remember, the Lord took only six days to create the world. If you haven't finished in six days, stay up all night, if necessary, to complete the job. If you haven't finished by morning, throw the rest in the trash. If there is anything left that is really important, you will find out about it eventually.

2. Throw all junk mail, unopened, into the trash on your way in from the mailbox, or order a rubber stamp that says, "Return to sender; remove name from mailing list!" and then use it.

3. Pay all bills immediately and put the check in a stamped, addressed envelope. Post, if necessary. If you don't have the money, write the check anyway and put these ready-to-be-mailed envelopes in a special place. Don't forget to deduct these amounts in your checkbook. You will simply have a minus number, which will always tell you how much you owe when your next check is deposited. It can even keep you from overspending.

4. If you have received any birth or wedding announcements, graduation or birthday party invitations, call a free shopping service at your local department store or use a mail-order catalog and order the gift immediately. If it is something you really must go out and buy, take out your calendar and schedule the time immediately. Record all necessary information with the note on your schedule and throw the invitation in the trash.

5. No matter how tired you are, or how late you get

home, complete all correspondence as well as filing, filling out forms, notes to the teacher, etc. before you go to bed. I promise it will be easier than when you have twice as much the next day.

6. Check your birthday and anniversary list, and select cards from a supply you have filed away.

That's it! That's all there is to it. I can't tell you how these six little rules have helped change my life. When you have a clean desk and you need to jot off a letter to one of your elected representatives, it's not a big deal, unless you are a victim of reason number two.

Reason number two is you're not quite sure how to write to your representatives and you don't want to do it wrong. The right way is covered in chapter 11, but I want to say right now that I don't think there is a wrong way. I think what we need are more notes scrawled on brown wrapping paper.

There is something more I'd like to add to the May Reser story. May had serious reservations about writing her first letter to Senator Armstrong because she is a Democrat and Armstrong a Republican. But not only did she write that letter, she also founded Disabled American Workers Security (DAWS) in 1982 and is now, at age 60, actively involved with this life-changing organization.

You are never too old, too insignificant, too handicapped or too busy that you can't make a difference!

How to Make Your Vote Equal 1,000

What's the difference between casting 1,000 ballots and persuading 1,000 people to vote your way on a candidate or issue? None. The end result is the same 1,000 votes.

The days of stuffing the ballot box are long gone, thank goodness. But today it is easier than ever before to persuade 1,000 people to think your way by using the two most accessible areas in the media, the editorial section of your local newspaper (via a letter-to-the-editor) and your local radio call-in talk show.

Here's your chance to present those clear, concise, well-organized facts to a good-sized audience. It's really much less threatening than making a speech, and can be much more effective. Best part of all, you can choose how, when and where. No credentials are required, everyone is invited to participate and, although newspapers usually print your name, on those radio talk shows you can be anonymous. So what have you got to lose?

Of course, the size of your audience will depend largely on the size of your city or town, but if you can articulate the facts on the issues you've studied, you'll find that, in most areas, 1,000 is a conservative estimate of people you will actually reach.

For example, the city of Tyler, Texas (pop. 125,000) has eight radio stations. During an average quarter-hour period from 6 A.M. to midnight, Monday through Sunday, approximately 10,900 people tune in to Tyler's most popular station, KNUE. During the same quarter hour, 600 people will listen to even the lowest-rated station in the market, KDOK.[18]

By looking at the audience numbers for Tyler, you can see just how popular radio is today and just what your potential audience is at any one time. If you live in Tyler, you can check with the individual stations to find out which ones have call-in shows and when they are on. The same is true in any other market.

I did some checking in Los Angeles, the second-largest city in the country. One of the most popular Christian stations there is KBRT. Rich Buhler has a call-in show from 2 to 6 P.M. daily. In the average quarter hour, approximately 16,700 people listen to that program.[19]

The most popular secular host of a radio call-in show in Los Angeles is Michael Jackson. His program is on from 9 A.M. to 1 P.M. local time. Approximately 136,000 people listen in any given quarter hour. The last two hours of the show are carried on the ABC Radio network, and if you're lucky enough to get through at that time, you will be heard by almost half a million people.[20]

ABC has affiliate stations all over the country, so even if you live in a small town, you still have an opportunity to be heard by a large audience by calling in to a network show.

You'll also find reaching 1,000 people by writing a letter-to-the-editor is a relatively conservative figure. In New York City, the *Daily News* is read by 4,468,300 people each day. In Wichita, Kansas, a much smaller city, the *Eagle Beacon* is read by approximately 324,100.[21] Of course, you can't expect the editorial portion to be scrutinized by all those folks. It will never compete with sports, comics or the want ads, but the editorial section is one of the most popular segments of any paper.

One advantage to using the letter-to-the-editor method of reaching people is that you can keep writing and rewriting your letter until you get it just the way you want it. You can even try it out on a few of your friends to make sure you get your point across. Then drop it into the mail box when you're ready.

Suzanne Clark was ready when she sent her letter-to-the-editor to her home town newspaper, the *Bristol* (Tennessee) *Herald Courier* on January 18, 1982. Suzanne, an

English teacher at a local Bible College, with a degree in creative writing from Johns Hopkins University, wrote her letter after reading an article published in that paper, written by the executive director of the National Education Association and the head of its Virginia affiliate, attacking the Reagan administration's education policies. Their article stated, "What, after all, could be more wholesome, cherished and even innocent than today's public school?"[22]

"That did it!" Suzanne said. "I just had to set the record straight. I didn't write it to create a stir." She accused the union of advocating atheistic humanism, the abolition of religion, sexual license and drug use. These things were abhorrent to her as a mother of two small children.[23]

The editor of the paper was so impressed with her letter that he asked to publish it as a guest article, which incensed the powerful teacher's union. The union demanded a retraction. When Suzanne refused, the National Education Association (NEA) sued her for $100,000. "I couldn't take it back," she explained. "I knew my statements were true."

Suzanne and her husband were ready to mortgage their home to provide the funds to defend the suit when Concerned Women for America (CWA)—an organization formed to preserve, protect and promote traditional and Judeo-Christian values—stepped in and raised the money for her defense (this further illustrates the advantage of belonging to one of these national organizations). After two years and over $70,000 in legal fees paid by CWA, the NEA gave up and dropped the suit just two weeks before the trial was to begin.

Suzanne accomplished quite a lot with that one letter. In pursuing the lawsuit, top NEA officials were forced to testify, under oath, about the union's activities in sex education, the nuclear freeze, opposition to creationism and prayer in schools. They were also forced to admit their financial and political involvement in a variety of noneducation related issues, including the promotion of the Equal Rights Amendment and federally funded abortions. [24]

The national media picked up the story, and the NEA lost membership[25] as literally thousands of Americans were made aware of the facts that Suzanne had presented in her original letter-to-the-editor.

You can do it, too.

How to Make Your Vote Equal 100,000

A recent film about young people in the '50s featured an argument between two adolescent boys over who was better, Mighty Mouse or Superman. "Mighty Mouse is just a cartoon character," one of the boys said. "Superman is real!"[26] That settled it. Superman was real to the boys because television had made him real. Any parent can appreciate that.

Television has become bigger than life itself. If it's on the tube, it must be so. Even as adults, we sometimes have trouble sorting out fact from fiction if it's on the nightly news.

Will Rogers, that great student of Americana, once said, "All I know is what I read in the papers."[27] If Will were around today, no doubt he would have contemporized that statement to, "All I know is what I see on television." More people can see than can read, and today they are seeing it more than ever before—on television.

If you can say it on the evening news or get someone else to say it for you, you can easily multiply your voice by influencing 100,000 or more viewers. When Dan Rather says it on the "CBS Evening News," he is watched by over 16 million people. [28]

Getting yourself or your opinion on a network news show is no small feat. But local news figures are equally staggering. WBBM in Chicago, the number three television market in the country, has over 820,000 people watching its nightly newscast. WPTA in Fort Wayne, Indiana, in market number 102, can produce over 70,000 viewers per newscast. [29]

It's no wonder that companies and organizations spend millions of dollars on public relations firms who have lots of high-priced account executives staying up late at night trying to figure out ways to get them a mention on these shows. Why do they do it?

David Brinkley had this to say about his profession: "The one function that TV news performs very well is that when there is no news we give it to you with the same emphasis as if there was news. [30] And like that young boy in the movie trying to explain Superman, millions of adults see it on television and say, "It must be so!"

10

How Does Our Government Work?

If you're going to take a trip in your car, you need a map; you also need one if you're going to get through the political process.

Maybe you're one of those people who resists maps. If not, you know the type. They use the box-of-rice method, dropping a grain here and there along the way so they can find their way back to where they started if they should get lost—and they frequently do. Every service station attendant in America can spot one of them coming. They drive in with a blank stare or a look of desperation and ask, "Can you tell me how to get to . . . ?" You can never quite convince them that reading a map *saves time*.

How Our Government Works

Here are a couple of "maps" to simplify your political journey. The first map (diagram 1) gives you the one- and two-way streets through our system of government. The second map (diagram 2) shows the road a piece of legislation must travel to become a law.

The most important thing we need to know about our government is that it is generally called a democracy. The word democracy comes from two Greek roots: *demos,* which means "people," and *kratos,* which means "rule." The literal meaning is "rule by the people."

A true democracy can only work in a small community, so our Constitution established a republican form of government, which means we elect fellow citizens to represent us in making laws. This achieves self-government, the goal of democracy for the people.

Jesus told us in Matthew 22:21 to: "Render therefore unto Caesar the things which are Caesar's; and unto God the things that are God's" *(KJV).* In a democracy, *we the people* are, in fact, Caesar. Do you see the implications for a Christian?

Our forefathers come here from many different backgrounds and cultures. Many fled from persecution to come to this new world, so they were extremely careful when they established our system of government. They set up an elaborate structure of checks and balances in an attempt to preserve their new found freedom.

JUDICIAL

When you look at the Balance of Powermap (diagram 1), you will notice that there is one branch of our government where we have no direct control—the judicial branch, headed by the Supreme Court. The nine Supreme Court justices are appointed by the president and, after confirmation by the Senate, they serve for life. They are charged with interpreting the Constitution, the law of the land.

The Supreme Court reviews decisions of lower federal

ONE AND TWO WAY STREETS
THROUGH OUR POLITICAL SYSTEM

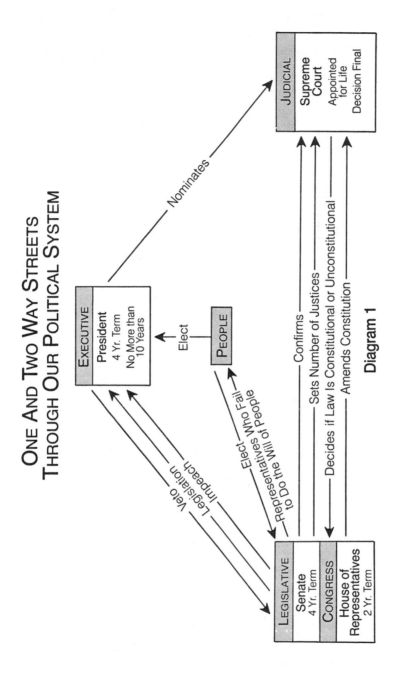

JUDICIAL

Supreme Court

Appointed for Life

Decision Final

EXECUTIVE

President

4 Yr. Term

No More than 10 Years

PEOPLE

Nominates

Elect

Confirms

Sets Number of Justices

Decides if Law Is Constitutional or Unconstitutional

Amends Constitution

Elect Who Fail — Representatives to Do the Will of People

Veto

Legislation

Impeach

LEGISLATIVE

Senate

4 Yr. Term

CONGRESS

House of Representatives

2 Yr. Term

Diagram 1

Road a Bill Must Travel to Become a Law

This graphic shows the most typical way in which proposed legislation is enacted into law. There are more complicated, as well as simpler, routes, and most bills fall by the wayside and never become law.

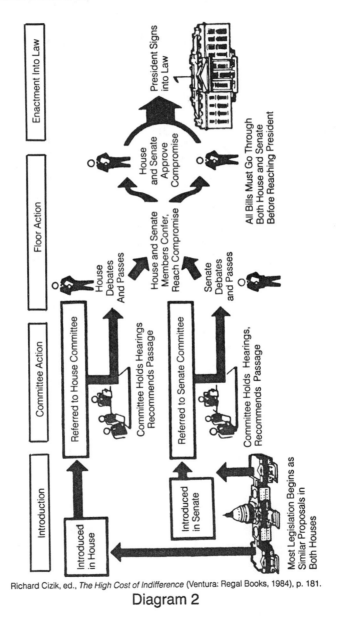

Richard Cizik, ed., *The High Cost of Indifference* (Ventura: Regal Books, 1984), p. 181.

Diagram 2

courts and the highest courts of the states. The Supreme Court also has the power to decide whether a federal or state law or executive action is constitutional. Supreme Court decisions are final. There is no appeal; however, the Supreme Court may reverse itself if it is convinced that an error has been made or a change in circumstance requires a different approach, but this doesn't happen very often. Thus, your only control over this branch is to elect a president who will appoint responsible people to one of these all-important positions as the need arises.

The Supreme Court's interpretation of the law does change occasionally. The changes are gradual and depend on the political, social and economic beliefs of the majority of its members, as well as national conditions at the time. Not every president has the opportunity to appoint a Supreme Court justice. When he does, it no doubt will be one of his most important decisions, because that appointment will have an effect on our country for years to come.

LEGISLATIVE

Our Constitution was framed on two basic principles: (1) that all states, regardless of size or population, would be equal; (2) that all people are equal. So, our founding fathers very cleverly set up two *houses* in Congress.

In the upper house, called the Senate, the states are equal. The Senate has 100 members, each state having two senators, who are elected for six-year terms. One third of the Senate body is elected every two years. Each senator is responsible to, and is elected by, all voters in his or her state. When a bill that concerns you comes up in the Senate, you will need to contact both of your state's senators.

The lower house in Congress, called the House of Representatives, was created to reflect population. The federal census determines each state's portion of its 435 representative seats. You have only one representative in the House of Representatives, elected by the voters in your immediate area. Because members of the House are responsible to a fewer number of voters and are elected for a short two-year term, you can easily see how these men and women are usually more accessible and generally more sensitive to your views than are senators.

Virtually everything we do is controlled by Congress because Congress is charged with making the laws by which we govern ourselves. This branch of government also controls our money through taxes and appropriations. In addition, Congress has the power to declare war; conduct investigations; impeach federal officials, including the president; monitor federal agencies; approve treaties; and confirm Supreme Court nominations and other top agency and military appointments.

How a Bill Becomes a Law

Any member of the House of Representatives or the Senate may introduce a bill—a proposed new law or a revision of an existing law. A bill may originate in either the House or the Senate, except those for raising revenue, which must start in the House of Representatives.

Many times, senators and representatives get together and introduce bills simultaneously. When bills are introduced, they are assigned a number with H or S in front of the number for House or Senate. It's important to have the correct number of a bill when you write to one of your representatives.

Even if two identical bills are introduced simultaneously, one in the House and one in the Senate, the road each must travel is long, hazardous and uncertain. They may be reworked and amended so many times that they may have little or no resemblance to the original bills by the time each is passed. And, of course, one or both may die along the way. In actuality, less than 5 percent of the bills that are introduced make it into law.[1]

Around 20,000 bills are introduced in an average two-year period. To handle the work load, each house of Congress is divided into committees. There are 22 permanent or standing committees in the House and 16 in the Senate.

The committees decide if the bill should be handled by the full committee or referred to a subcommittee. A detailed study is then made. Your input is very important at this time. If you want a particular bill to pass, you should follow it along this road and request a full and respectful hearing at this stage by writing to the committee's office. You can locate that address in the *Congressional Directory* at your local library or through the office of your congressman. You can also obtain a copy of the *U.S. Congressional Handbook* by writing Box 566, McLean, VA 22101.

If a bill has been referred to a subcommittee and a majority approves, the bill goes back to the full committee. This is another important time to make your voice heard. If your own congressman happens to be on the subcommittee, a well-written letter could make a difference in the bill's outcome, because committee members may amend the bill as they wish. The bill must then be approved by the majority of the committee before it can go back to the House or Senate floor. Only 10 percent make it that far.

If a committee fails to report the bill, by sending it back to the House or Senate floor for a vote, the bill is usually dead at that point. However, the bill can be forced out of committee in the House by a discharge petition signed by a majority of the full membership. The same goal can be accomplished by motion in the Senate. This practice is rarely done, but it does prevent a committee from burying a controversial measure.

When a bill is reported out by a committee, it is then placed on the calendar for consideration by the full House of Representatives or the Senate. It is vitally important to contact your representative(s) just before the vote. Once again, the full House or Senate can amend (change) the bill again before this vote. The bill can even be postponed at this point and sent back to the committee for more study.

When a bill is passed by one house, it then goes to the other for consideration; but even when both houses have passed a bill, more changes may occur.

Because the House and Senate versions are seldom identical, it must go to a joint conference committee, which must come up with a final version. It must then be voted on as is by each house or sent back to the joint committee to be reworked once again.

When the final version is passed by the House and the Senate, it then goes to the president. When the bill reaches the president's desk, he has three choices: (1) he can sign it into law; (2) he can let it sit on his desk for 10 days and it becomes law automatically; or (3) he can veto the bill. Even then, the bill can be passed over his veto by a two-thirds vote of each house, but this is rarely done.[2]

EXECUTIVE BRANCH

Our president is sometimes called the *chief of state*. He is often compared to an elected monarch, but there are few kings or queens at this time who have as much authority. He holds several titles simultaneously, which are often split between two or more people in monarchies and parliamentary democracies. He also performs many of the same functions as a prime minister.

As chief executive, the president presides over the cabinet, comprised of the secretaries of the several executive departments. The cabinet is an institution based on custom, not law. It was created for the purpose of giving advice and support—how much advice and support depends on the wishes of the president.

Our president is the commander in chief of the army and navy, and the state militias as well, when they are called into the service of the country. Even though Congress has the power to declare war, the president has the authority to protect the United States from sudden attack and to initiate military activities without a formal declaration of war.

In addition to Supreme Court justices, the president also nominates/appoints ambassadors, public ministers and consuls, and a host of other federal officials.

The president is instructed by the Constitution to periodically inform Congress on the state of the union and recommend necessary and expedient legislation.

As you might imagine, the president's influence in the legislative process depends largely on whether his political party has a majority in the House or Senate. His recommendations, however, are always newsworthy and cannot easily be ignored.

The president is elected by all the eligible voters in the United States. Since there are so many of us, your chances of any direct contact with the president are pretty remote, but it is important that you let him know your views. The pressure from special interest groups is always intense, so the White House welcomes and encourages your input and response. There is even a special public opinion phone number that you can use on all immediate issues—(202) 456-7639—but, when time allows, a letter is always the most effective means of communication.

The important thing is that we *do* converse with our elected officials—all of them. Interestingly enough, the Greek word from which we get the English word *politics* can be translated "conversation."

How Political Parties Work

"It makes no difference who you vote for—the two parties are really one party representing 4 percent of the people."[3] That statement by Gore Vidal may be a bit of an *under*exaggeration, but it's not as far off as you might imagine.

A political party is an organized group of people who control, or seek to control, a government. In democracies, political parties compete against each other. In the United States, we have two major political parties, the Democratic and Republican parties. There have been many other smaller parties in this country from time to time. None of them was ever strong enough to win a presidential election, but many of their proposals gained such widespread support that the major parties were forced to adopt them.

If you are really serious about making a difference and have limited time to spend, you might consider working for one of our nation's two major political parties.

"Wait a minute!" you're probably saying to yourself. "You just said *if* you have limited time to spend, and you're talking about working for a political party?"

That's right, if you want to get the most value for minutes spent, you'll find this is one of the fastest ways to have your views reflected in our nation's government.

Every four years our attention is focused on the national conventions of the two major political parties. Each party brings about 2,000 delegates together for the purpose of nominating a candidate for president of the United States. These delegates also decide on the party's platform—that means they decide what stand that party will take on the issues of the day. Imagine that! Around 2,000 people are making decisions that could affect the whole country for the next four years!

Who are these delegates that weigh such important matters? They are people, just like you and me, who have taken the time to work and get involved on the local level. Believe it or not, all it takes is a phone call to your local party headquarters. Just tell whoever answers the phone that you'd like to get involved. Party leaders are always looking for willing volunteers.

If there is a local party meeting, attend with several of your friends. Local issues are often discussed and you may have an opportunity to give some input right away. What probably will happen is that you will have an opportunity to volunteer and will be assigned a small task, such as registering voters, serving on a committee or serving as a poll watcher in your precinct.

Whatever job you are assigned, do it well. This is your chance to prove yourself, and in no time at all you will be regarded as a valuable party member. You may even be appointed or elected to your city or county central committee or governing body. After some length of service, you may have an opportunity to be one of those delegates yourself on the state or national level.

Remember, if Christians aren't willing volunteers, they leave these valuable positions open to those with other philosophies and agendas. The opportunity is there for each one of us. Will you take it?

Why not have a little election in your own family or prayer group? Decide which one of you would make the best party volunteer and have the others support that person. Give everyone a job, such as writing letters, studying the issues or performing the household chores of the other family member when he or she is pressed into service.

If Christians are so involved in their churches and families that they are too busy, who does it leave to determine our fate? If *we the people* are Caesar, can we refuse to govern ourselves and expect to be held blameless before our Maker?

11
How Can I Put It In Writing?

What is an effective letter? One that gets the attention and action of your elected representative. That's not an easy thing to do. Consider the sheer volume of mail that is delivered daily to the House and Senate office buildings.

The most common attention getter is the poster-sized letter. Most people feel the bigger, the better. A few are so big and so clever they've literally hung around for years, decorating the walls of various congressional offices. These don't come in the mail. They must be hand-delivered by the writer or a local messenger service. Another approach that seems to be getting more popular is the recorded letter on cassette tape—audio and video. Some people even put their message to music, and a few folks have gone to the trouble to include the recorder along with the tape so all the busy representative has to do is push-play. If you're a creative type, you might use some of these suggestions. Just make sure your message is as weighty as its package.

Almost everyone on Capitol Hill has a favorite mail room story, from messages written on shoe soles, grocery bags, blocks of wood, to an umbrella with holes cut in the fabric on the subject of acid rain.

Francis Marcus, in the office of North Carolina Senator Jesse Helms, told me that in one campaign people literally sent in their *two cents* worth. "We didn't know what to do with all those pennies. We tried to send them back but it was impossible!"

She also said Senator Helms, who is extremely sensitive to the mail and well known for his wit, often comes in on Saturdays and picks letters at random to answer personally. Her favorite reply was one that Helms sent to a constituent who had done nothing but berate Helms in his letter. The senator's answer was a simple one-liner: "I hope you feel better."

Getting attention is one thing, but getting the action you want is something quite different.

Organized campaigns often are effective because of the sheer volume of mail they deliver and the workload they create. A few years ago, when banks were required to withhold taxes from savings account, they handed out form letters of complaint to send to representatives in Congress, which tied up the legislative office staffs answering all those letters. The law was repealed quickly.

How Can I Put It in Writing?

But you don't have to live in Washington, have the money to afford a messenger service or be particularly creative or funny to make a difference, because the individual, well-written letter is still the most powerful means of communication.

Brian Gunderson, a legislative assistant in the office of Congressman Dick Armey of Texas, told me the thing that surprised him the most when he first went to work on Capitol Hill was "just how much the mail means. If we get as few as five letters from individuals on one piece of legislation, it gets our attention. We don't just answer the mail and say, 'thank you for your letter,' we draft a position paper."

To draft a position paper, the staff really has to research the issue in order to present the facts to its senator or representative so that he or she can make an informed decision on the issue. If you have included a newspaper clipping or mentioned a study or two, the staff has something to follow up on. This can be extremely helpful to your cause.

Gunderson, who is in charge of correspondence for Armey, had a few suggestions for making sure your letter has impact. "The most important thing to remember is make them legible. You'd be surprised how often we receive letters we just can't read." He also pointed out that it is extremely important to mention the bill number so the staff can be sure it knows exactly which issue you are discussing.

Good suggestions! Here are some others from key people in charge of correspondence in the various legislative offices on Capitol Hill:

1. *Be specific.* Write about only one issue per letter. Each legislative assistant is assigned different issues. Since your letter most likely will be routed to the assistant who handles the first issue you mention, the second issue may be lost entirely.

2. *Be selective.* Concentrate on your own delegation. If you send a letter to a representative of another state or

district, his or her office staff most likely will forward it to your own representative.

3. *Be brief.* No one wants to wade through a lengthy letter. A letter longer than a page is often skimmed and your main points may be lost.

4. *Be courteous.* Use the correct form of address for your elected representative (see list later in this chapter and include your name and address on the letter, as well as on the envelope).

5. *Be personal.* Write in your own words. Avoid copying form letters or using stilted language. Explain how the issue will affect you, your children, your family, school, business, community and so on.

6. *Be informed.* Don't rely on rumors or hearsay. Get your facts straight and, whenever possible, enclose clippings from newspapers, magazines or your organization's newsletter.

7. *Be timely.* Follow the issue in the newsletters you receive and keep up with the day-to-day developments in the paper. The best time to write is when you first hear the issue is going to be considered. You may encourage your representative to take the right position before the opposition gets to him or her.

8. *Be supportive.* After the vote is taken, write and say thanks if you feel your representative voted correctly.

9. *Be tenacious.* Ask specific questions that must be answered by a person, not a computer. Keep copies of your correspondence and be prepared to send a follow-up letter if necessary. When an elected official has

adopted a position in conflict with yours, you often will get a letter of explanation. This may be your best opportunity. Politely refute the arguments presented in the reply you receive with as many facts as you can muster.

Here are some important don'ts to remember:

1. Don't use threatening language or be hostile, abusive or disrespectful in any way.

2. Don't try to convert your representative to your religion. You want to influence his voting patterns.

3. Don't use form letters.

4 Don't be afraid to point out your expertise. So few letters come from someone who has real experience with an issue. These letters are extremely valuable to a congressman and the staff.

5. Don't be a pen pal. You're after quality, not quantity. By all means, write on the issues you feel are important, but don't weigh down the mail every few days with volumes on every conceivable subject.

6. Don't fail to write because you're afraid of doing it wrong. The most important thing to remember is, as long as you're sincere and polite, there is no wrong way to write a letter to one of your representatives.

Forms of Address

President

President (first and last name)
The White House
Washington, DC 20500

Dear Mr. or Madam President:
Very respectfully,

Vice President

Vice President (first and last name)
The White House
Washington, DC 20501

Dear Mr. or Madam Vice President:
Sincerely yours,

Members of Cabinet
(except Attorney General)

The Honorable (first and last name)
The Secretary of (name of Cabinet post)
Washington, DC (See below for zip code)

Dear Mr. or Madam Secretary:
Sincerely yours,

Important Note

Each Cabinet member has a different zip code:

Agriculture: 20250
CIA Director: 20505
Commerce: 20230
Defense: 20301
Education: 20202
Energy: 20585
Health and Human Services: 20201
Housing and Urban Development: 20410
Interior: 20240
Labor: 20210
State: 20520
Transportation: 20590
Treasury: 20220
UN Ambassador: 799 United Nations Plaza,
                          New York, NY 10017

Attorney General

The Attorney General
Washington, DC 20530

Dear Mr. or Madam Attorney General:
Sincerely yours,

Senators

The Honorable (first and last name)
United States Senate
Washington, DC 20510

Dear Senator (last name):
Sincerely yours,

Representatives

The Honorable (first and last name)
House of Representatives
Washington, DC 20515

Dear Congressman or Congresswoman (last name):
or
Dear Mr., Mrs. or Miss (last name):
Sincerely yours,

Judiciary

The Honorable (full name)
Associate Justice (or Chief Justice)
United States Supreme Court
Washington, DC 20543

Dear Mr. or Madam Justice: or Dear Mr. or Madam
Justice (last name):
Sincerely yours,

Letters to justices of the Supreme Court or other judges should be written after a case is decided. This may appear unproductive to you, but most judges will not read their mail concerning an undecided issue until after the decision.

Then why write?

Michael Farris, a Washington attorney with the Home School Legal Defense Association, spotted Justice Byron White in the Dulles Airport with his wife in the fall of 1986, a few months after Justice White had written the majority opinion on the Bowers Case, which upheld Georgia's sodomy laws. Farris approached Justice White and thanked him profusely. He went on to say, "I thought it was a tremendous decision and I'm proud of what you've done!"

Justice White gave him a very tired look and said, "You're probably the only person in America who thinks so." No doubt, when the next sodomy case comes before the high court, those kind words from Michael Farris will go a long way toward encouraging Justice White as he remembers all those angry letters he received. Judges are human and need positive reinforcement, just like the rest of us.

Sample Letter

Dear Senator Smith:

Identify one topic with bill number.
I am writing to express my opposition to S.J. Res. 1, known as The Equal Rights Amendment.

Use because paragraph.
I am appalled that the Senate is using its valuable time to debate this worn-out piece of bad legislation once again.

Give your qualifications, if applicable.
I was a successful commercial artist for five years before taking time out to raise a family. During those five years I

had no trouble competing with men with similar training and ability.

State how it will affect you personally.
The ERA, as it is written, poses too many uncertainties. Will my daughters be drafted into the military one day on an equal basis with men? Will girls' athletic teams still exist when my children enter college? Will my tax money be used for federally funded abortions? I would much rather these and other related issues be dealt with responsibly by you and other elected members of Congress rather than the High Court, which is answerable to no one.

Use expert opinion and literature with facts and figures.
Dean Pound of the Harvard Law School has stated, "If anything about this proposed amendment is clear, it is that it would transform every provision of law concerning women into a constitutional issue to be ultimately resolved by the Supreme Court of the United States."[1] I'm sure you are familiar with the analysis of this amendment written by Senator Orrin Hatch who chaired the Subcommittee on the Constitution when the amendment was re-introduced in Congress in 1982. I am enclosing a copy for your review in case you do not have it in your personal library.

State how you would like him/her to vote and request response. After carefully studying this issue, I feel that passing the ERA would be like asking the women of America to take an experimental drug, and then saying, "It *might* help you, but we're not sure, and there are *unknown* side effects." I urge you to speak out against S.J. Res. 1 and vote against the ERA if it is reported out of committee. Please let me know how you intend to vote.

Thank you in advance for your careful consideration on this issue.

Sincerely yours,

Mrs. Anne Jones

Now Is the Time

If you've never written to one of your elected representatives, now is the time to take out your pen and paper and try it yourself. If you don't know if there is any legislation in progress on one of your issues, then contact one of the organizations listed in the appendices of this book to find out. If you're already a member of one or more of these groups, check the newsletters. If you have trouble getting started, just tell yourself you're going to write the letter only to see what it will be like. You don't have to mail it if you're not happy when you finish. The important thing is to try it—and to finish.

You can see just how simple it is to write an effective letter when you break it down into the five or six paragraphs shown in the example. If you need help with a few facts and figures, just refer to the issue section of this book. Remember, you are an expert because almost every issue that comes before Congress will affect you in a very personal way.

Other Forms that Get Quick Results

If one of your issues is coming up for a vote in Congress or your state legislature and you really haven't time to draft a letter, don't miss an opportunity to let your voice be heard just because you can't write. If your elected representative doesn't have a deep personal conviction on the issue coming up for a vote, usually the last thing he or she does is check the mail and phone calls from the folks back home. It's a numbers game.

Seize the moment and employ one of the following:

Telegrams, Mailgrams, and Opiniongrams

These timely messages carry quite an impact and usually end up right on your representative's desk. If you've got the money to spend, they can be a good investment.

The opiniongram was created just to allow you to get those important messages to your elected representatives immediately, using their telex system. The cost is $4.45 for the first 20 words and $2.00 for each additional 20 words.

The old fashioned telegram is $8.75 for 10 words or less, 45 cents for each additional word, and another $9.75 to have it delivered, usually within two to five hours.

If you have a lot to say in a hurry, the mailgram is your best bet: 50 words for $9.75, $2.95 for each additional 50 words, and it is delivered in the next day's mail.

Telephone Calls

The telephone is the most economical way to express your opinion when you find out that a vote on an issue you feel strongly about is coming up right away. Just call your representative's local office. It's the total number of calls that can make a difference, so be sure to share this information with your friends and get them to call, also. Be sure to give the bill number and ask to be informed on how your representative voted.

If you've got some important information on the issue or would simply like to say a little more, then call the Washington office—or state office for assemblyman or state senator—and ask to speak to the legislative assistant who handles that issue. Make some notes for yourself and follow the same guidelines as for letter writing. Be brief and courteous.

Postcards

Never underestimate the value of a postcard. When you're too busy to write a letter, a personal postcard is the next best thing when you have enough time to get your message to your elected representative by mail.

By now, you've probably been exposed to the impersonal postcard, the kind that comes in the mail from organizations you have joined. It already has the name and address of your elected representative on the front and a message printed on the back. All you have to do is put your name and address on it, stamp it and toss it in the mail.

Mailing one of these is a lot better than doing nothing at all. But if you'll keep a supply of postcards with pictures on the front of your city and write your own message on the back, it's so much more effective. That way the staff in Washington knows for sure it's from a *real live person* back home. Better still, you might find some funny ones with an eye-catching cartoon on the front. These get the attention of the staff and are often placed right on the legislator's desk so that he or she can have a chuckle, too.

How to Write a Letter to the Editor

The best way to get the attention of any public official is to mention his or her name in a letter to the editor of a magazine or newspaper. This is especially true of your elected representatives. They are extremely sensitive to what is said about them in the local papers. You can be sure if you mention their names and the letters get printed, those letters will be clipped and sent directly to the representatives' desks.

Writing a letter to the editor of a national news magazine is an excellent way to get your message directly to the president or a member of his cabinet or any other high ranking government official. The letter-to-the-editor section is one of the most widely read parts of any paper or magazine.

Getting your letter printed is not as easy as you might imagine. It, too, is a numbers game, so it's a good idea to get several of your friends to write letters at the same time. The folks that put that section together usually tabulate the letters they receive on each subject and then select a representative number from the most popular issues.

Before you begin, be sure to check the publication's printed guidelines for letter writing and follow them. They are usually printed right on the page with the letters. Always type your letter. Newspapers and magazines receive so many they are not likely to wade through one that is handwritten. Here are some other suggestions:

1. The address and salutation should always be *Letter to the Editor*.
2. If you are responding to a previous editorial, article or

letter, state the title, name of the author and date at the beginning of your letter.

3. Strike while the issue is hot. Respond to the issue within a day or two to have the best chance of getting your letter in print.
4. Cover only one topic in a letter.
5. Be as brief as you can and still make your point.
6. Whenever possible, include factual evidence to support your claim. Short quotations are good, but longer ones may be deleted.
7. Whenever possible, use humor. Anger is all right, but avoid hysteria or you will lose your credibility.
8. Offer a positive solution or end with a good, solid punch line.
9. Always sign your letter and include your address and phone number.

Here are some examples of letters that made some good points and got those points in print.

The American Civil Liberties Union is again guilty of distorting the issue of pornography by claiming that Meese plans to divert "serious law-enforcement efforts to little skirmishes against 'dirty' books." More accurately, he is responding to millions of Americans who view law-enforcement efforts against obscene materials as a very serious priority. The main thrust will be against major hard-core distributors backed by organized crime—hardly "little skirmishes." Further, obscenity today involves more than dirty books. It involves brutal fare on videocassettes, cable, telephone wires, computers, in magazines and increasingly seeping into radio and network TV. Meese's plans come none too soon.

Betty Wein
New York City

U.S. NEWS & WORLD REPORT, Nov. 17, 1986
Used by permission.

Uninformed Consent

Kirk Bingham misses the point in his letter in the Nov. 24 issue. With thousands of families across the country unable to adopt a child, no baby is unwanted.

Furthermore, numerous studies have shown that women who have abortions can have a higher risk of complications in later pregnancies. Women can also experience mental anguish over the abortion. In no other medical procedure is a patient given so little information about possible physical and mental outcomes associated with the procedure.

Susan Jordan
Fountain Valley, Calif.

INSIGHT Dec. 22, 1986
Used by permission.

Textbook war: It is about time American parents closely examine the textbooks our children are studying. I have read Dr. Paul Vitz's Education Department study, referred to in "The Textbook Tug of War Heats Up" (November 17). It is not a casual, accidental overlooking of traditional family values, but a methodical, conscious effort.

When 30 pages can be devoted to the Pilgrims in a social-studies text without mention of the historical fact that they came to this nation to exercise religious freedom, something is wrong.

Michael G. O'Callaghan
Allegan, Mich.

U.S. NEWS & WORLD REPORT, Dec. 1, 1986
Used by permission.

Don't get discouraged if your letter is not printed. It still will have an impact. Letters to the editor show the interest level on a given issue. The number of letters received on an issue has a direct relationship to the amount of space and coverage devoted to the subject in the future.

GIVE A LETTER-WRITING PARTY

This is a good way to respond to a new bill that has just been introduced or stir up some action on one that is coming up for a vote. Invite your friends and make it fun. Have a good supply of newspaper and magazine articles to hand out. You can do this in a hurry by running down to your library and using the *Reader's Guide to Periodical Litera-*

ture. Just look under your subject and you will find a list of all the articles written on the relevant issue over the last few years. You can go to the magazine files and make copies. Also there should be a guide to one or two newspapers available.

Begin with a general briefing on the issue. You may want to include an audiotape or videotape that can be ordered from one of the organizations listed in the appendices of this book. Then distribute copies of the articles. It's a good idea to give each person a different story if you can. Have a good supply of different kinds of stationery available, or ask your friends to bring their own. Have one or two typewriters on hand for writing letters to the editor.

When everyone is finished, read the letters and give prizes for the best letters in different categories: most original, most persuasive, best use of humor, etc.

As your friends leave, pass out stamps, but have every person mail his or her own letter. It's best if letters are mailed from several different postal zones and on several different days. You may want to include a regular time for letter writing once a month at the end of a meeting of your local club or prayer group. Think of what could be accomplished if you could change people with good intentions to people who take action!

In a 1984 Louis Harris poll, 1,008 shoppers were asked this question: *How do you personally feel about writing letters to your congressman?*

19 percent said they had written.
22 percent said they were ready to write.
37 percent said they sympathized but wouldn't write.

17 percent said it would be ineffective.
5 percent said they weren't sure.[2]

If you go over all the survey data for the last decade, you'll find many polls have asked the question, "Have you written to a representative, Congressman or Senator?" Twenty percent is the most who have said they have ever written. That means that those 22 percent who say they're getting ready to write never seem to get around to it. They're always just getting ready. Don't be one of them. Always be ready.

12
ME? GO PUBLIC?

Have you ever visited our nation's Capitol? If your answer is yes, did you visit with your representative or your state's senators? A lot of folks do. The staffs eagerly welcome constituents—that's what they call the people who live in their district or state. They are anxious to do everything possible to make their visits more enjoyable and to send them back home with favorable impressions.

Most of the people who stop by are seeking tourist information and passes to the House and Senate visitors' galleries. Special tours of the White House and some executive agencies often are arranged.

FACE-TO-FACE WITH YOUR ELECTED REPRESENTATIVE: LOBBYING

Many constituents make appointments in advance and meet their legislators—senators or representative—personally, but only a few actually use this time to do anything more than shake hands and exchange pleasantries. What a shame, when you consider this is often your best opportunity to share ideas and information on an important issue! It is the only time you can be absolutely sure your message gets to your legislators unaltered.

When you use this visit with one of your legislators to discuss an issue and try to influence his or her vote, it's called *lobbying*. That's all there is to it. You don't have to be registered or on somebody's payroll or a member of a special interest group. In fact, you can be far more effective than professional lobbyists because you have the power to vote in the legislator's state or district, and you have a circle of influence in your town or city.

It's vitally important that we take the time to do this as often as we can because our legislators are insulated by their staffs, who often filter through what they want the boss to see or hear. If the legislative assistant who handles your issue has strong feelings that conflict with yours, you have two choices: you can educate the legislative assistant or you can deliver a few well-chosen words personally. Why not do both?

Here's a checklist:

1. Well in advance of your trip to Washington, call or write for appointments. Get the names of the legislative assistants who handle your issues.

2. Get as much information on your legislators as possible. Ask the staffs to send you biographies and their voting records on the issues that are important to you. If you have trouble obtaining voting records, check the resource organizations in the appendices of this book.

3. Well before your visit, write at least one letter on each issue you would like to discuss and study the replies. If your legislators don't agree with you on an issue, they

probably will give you the concerns they have on your point of view.

4. You can expect about 15 minutes with your senator or representative, so select only one or two issues at the most that have current legislation pending and prepare for your meeting.

5. Follow up with a phone call or letter to the appropriate legislative assistant. Ask for an appointment with him or her before your scheduled appointment time with your senator or representative.

6. Select one or two pieces of written material dealing with your legislator's concerns on the issue to hand to him or her during the meeting. Highlight the main points. Make a copy for the legislative assistant.

7. Practice with a friend. Role-play and try to cover all your main points in five minutes. Then switch roles. Try to see the issue from your legislator's point of view and ask yourself, What could someone say that might cause me to reconsider this issue?

You may find that your representative and senators agree with you on your issues, though it is unlikely this will happen with all three. Take the time to meet with those who share your views. Remember, they are being lobbied vigorously by the other side and need to hear from you. Affirm them. Thank them. Share information and ask what you might do for them to help out back home.

Here are some things to remember during your visit:

1. Arrive a little early. Remember, your elected representatives are very busy people. If you are late, you might not be able to see them at all.

2. Spend no more than two or three minutes on the

greeting. If you waste precious minutes on hometown chatter, your elected representative will be out the door and gone before you've even had a chance to bring up your issue, much less discuss it.

3. Tell your legislator how much you appreciate the time it took to explain in writing his or her position on the issue you came to discuss, and explain that you would like to go over these points and share some information. Use charts, diagrams and any other printed material you have to make your points quickly.

4. Ask if there are any other factors that have contributed to his or her position on the issue. You will learn how to proceed by asking questions.

5. Ask your legislator to go over your material and get back to you after taking the time to reconsider his or her position.

6. If you are asked a question that you cannot answer, offer to obtain the information, and then do so as soon as possible.

7. Follow up with a letter of thanks to your representative and/or senators and to the legislative assistants and, if possible, enclose more information on the issues previously discussed.

If you cannot go to Washington for a personal visit, it is possible to lobby right in your own state. The average representative makes 35 trips home during the year for official functions and meetings with constituents. Call the local office and ask for a schedule and an appointment.

If you plan to make your visit with a spouse or friend, work out your five-minute strategy ahead of time. Decide which one of you will take the lead. The other should be ready to offer back-up material and support, if necessary. You'll find this same plan of action will work with all of your elected officials, from your elected state officials to the local dog catcher, if necessary.

Don't forget the most important part of your preparation is practice. This shouldn't be too hard. After all, your goal is to educate and inform. The opportunities are all around you. Practice on a friend who has never studied your issue. Practice on a friend who has and is on the other side of your issue.

FACE TO FACE WITH AN AUDIENCE: SPEECHMAKING

If you have taken that step and discussed an issue with a friend or one of your elected representatives, do you realize what you've done? You've made a speech. Ah, but I was only talking to one person, you might say.

My dictionary says a speech is a talk made to an audience. How many people make up an audience? It doesn't say. It could be just one. In fact, the very best speechmakers talk as if they are speaking to just one person. Have you ever noticed that? The more intimate and direct the person making the speech is, the more you can relate and enjoy what the speechmaker has to say.

If the speechmaker is cold and aloof, if he or she tries to impress you with credentials, big words or technical jargon you don't understand, you can bet it's because of insecurity and inexperience.

The best way I know to give a speech is to speak as if you were talking to your very best friend. In fact, if your very best friend is *really* your very best friend, he or she may consent to be your first audience.

The Organization
Now, you're probably saying to yourself, How can you

say I made a speech by just talking to one of my elected representatives or to a friend? I prepared only five minutes of important facts about my issue. Well, that was the body of a speech, the main points or essence of what you would want to cover if you had an opportunity to address a large audience on the subject. You might want to include just a few more facts or perhaps a brief history of the issue you are discussing, but that's basically all you need. Add an opening and a close and you've got it!

Don't worry about having enough material. Did you ever hear someone complain about a speech being too short? Conversely, you can have the greatest speech in the world and go too long and completely lose your audience. As they say in show biz, "Leave 'em wanting more!"

I would be less than honest if I didn't tell you that the opening and close are the most difficult parts of a speech to prepare, and the most important. But there are some simple rules you can follow that will put you in safe territory and insure that your first official speech is a success.

The Opening

Regardless of what you may have heard or experienced, don't begin with a funny story unless you're a natural comic. Even if you are, this can be dangerous on your first few attempts at speechmaking. There are just too many things that can go wrong. What if the audience has already heard your funny story? This is one common mistake of fledgling speakers.

The Anecdote Opening. The easiest, most foolproof way to begin is to start with an anecdote that illustrates the main point or theme of what you have to say. It can be about yourself, it can be about someone you know or someone you've only read about. Perhaps you can begin by asking yourself why this issue is so important to you now. It could be because you've been affected in a very personal way. If your topic is abortion, maybe you've had one or have a friend who's had one. If you haven't, get a copy of *Every Woman Has a Right to Know the Dangers of Legal Abortion*. It's listed in the appendices of this book. You could begin with a story from that book. Make it come alive for your audience.

The Current Event Opening. A first cousin to the anecdote is the current event. Pick one that is so recent and so big that almost everyone in your audience will know something about it. As you speak, each person immediately can relate to what you are saying and will start to bring up their own mental image of the incident.

The Question Opening. Another good way to begin is by asking questions that will bring about an unqualified yes from your audience. It's not necessary that the response be verbal, but you can ask for a show of hands or some other sign if you feel comfortable with that. No matter how big the issue or how wide the differences, there always are points on which everyone can agree. Begin with those points. When you know your audience is with you, raise some questions and proceed with the answers.

The Startling Opening. If you have a flair for drama, then you can begin with one simple, startling statement or question, followed by a pause. Then proceed to explain the facts surrounding your statement and how they relate to the issue at hand. This involves perfect timing, and must be practiced over and over again.

The Ending

While the opening must be perfectly orchestrated to capture the attention of the audience, the ending must be forceful enough to drive home your theme. One or two good lines is all it takes, but they must be carefully rehearsed and delivered with a flourish.

Remember the advice of the king in *Alice in Wonderland?* "Begin at the beginning. Go on till you come to the end: then stop."[1] Those practical directions work well in almost any endeavor, but when preparing a speech you might find it helpful to *begin* at the *end.*

Once you have your topic or theme, you can simply ask yourself, "What's the one thing I want these folks to remember?" Perhaps you already have a powerful statement that has served you well. Put it down on paper and examine it. Will it work with this crowd, in this situation? If it does, go back to the beginning and work toward that ending. That's not as crazy as it may seem. Would you get on a train or plane without knowing the destination?

Here are some other suggestions that you can use effectively:

Repeat your opening. Perhaps you have a speech to deliver on comparable worth and you want to begin with the question, "What would your standard of living be if we did away with the free market system?" At the end of your speech, you could pause, look at your audience and say, "What would your standard of living be if we did away with the free market system?"

Ask for action. Make it simple and direct. "As you leave, each of you take a petition, and don't rest until you have it filled with the signatures of the people who live on your street. Let's work together and rid our neighborhood of this adult bookstore!"

Summarize your main points. When I first began writing news copy I was given this advice: Tell them. Tell them what you told them and then tell them again! The points you've just made may be crystal clear in your own mind, but consider the amount of time you have put into this issue. The material you just dished out may be so new to your audience that it simply won't stay with them unless you summarize. If it's good material, they'll want to remember it and will welcome the summary. Make it brief, bright and lively.

Finish with a prophesy. "If we fail to act now to defend our freedoms, before long there will be nothing left upon which to act."

Use emotional appeal. End with a powerful example. Draw in the audience. You might do this by using the name of a person in the example you just gave and saying something like, "There's an Anna in your church, in your neighborhood, on your street; maybe tomorrow there will be an Anna in your own family. Can you afford to give? You can't afford not to!"

Did you notice how that last sentence ended with a preposition? That's enough to incur the wrath of more than one of my English teachers. The point I want to make is, a speech is meant for the ear, not the eye. It should be prepared and delivered the way you speak—not the way anyone else speaks—because you're the one delivering it. Poring over a thesaurus and putting in a lot of eloquent language isn't going to help your credibility—it will only make you into a caricature.

A famous story is told about Winston Churchill. While occupying one of his earlier ministerial posts in the British government he had to submit his speeches to various department heads for approval. One of his speeches came back all marked up by an overzealous critic who had altered a number of sentences because each ended with a preposition. An enraged Churchill returned it with these words scrawled in the margin, "This is the sort of English up with which I will not put."[2] The grammarian had completely destroyed the rhythm and flow of his talk!

The Goal

Your goal is to educate and inform, not to impress. When you keep this goal firmly in your mind, your focus will be on the people who make up your audience. That's the best way to eliminate stage fright. A person who is self-conscious is thinking about self. Mentally wrap your arms around your audience, love them, enjoy them, appreciate them and send them away with some valuable information. That's all there is to it.

If you find that your heart is speeding up and your breathing is faster just before you get up to speak, don't be alarmed. That's nature's way of preparing you to go into action. It means your mind is alert and you have energy to spare. You can spring to the podium! Dale Carnegie pointed out that speakers who say they are as cool as a cucumber at all times are usually about as inspiring as one.

The Preparation

The best way to prepare your talk is to make a few notes or an outline, if you're comfortable doing that. Write a few words on each point, just enough to jog your memory. When you have something that you want to tell a friend, you don't think about what words you will use. You just tell them. The words come naturally. One small piece of paper should be sufficient. If you have some facts and figures or a poem you want to share, you can carry them with you on separate sheets of paper.

If you're absolutely convinced that you can't put two

words together, then write it all out. Take a good look. Read it over a couple of times if you must, and then give it to a friend or your spouse and make him or her promise not to give it back until after your speech. You can file it away for reference.

Then prepare from your notes or outline. The most dangerous thing you can do is try to memorize a speech, because one of two things will happen. You'll either forget it or your delivery will be dull. If your mind is occupied with trying to remember the exact words, you can't speak from the heart and you'll be incapable of an original thought.

The Delivery

Voice. Think about keeping it low in pitch. If the tension level is high, your voice tends to be high also. This is not pleasing to the ear and will make it more difficult for your words to be digested. It's a good idea to practice with a tape recorder. Every time you play back a rehearsal you will hear things you'd like to improve and you can begin to make adjustments. Also, it will give you practice with a microphone. Don't crowd the mike. It distorts your voice. You will also need to keep some distance between your mouth and the mike so that you can vary your force and volume for emphasis.

Feet. If you are a man, begin with your feet lined up directly under your shoulders. This way you are balanced and will be free to gesture or move about at any moment. For a woman, I think it is much more flattering to have one foot slightly in front of the other in the pedestal stance. The heel of the back foot should be turned slightly in toward the body so that both feet form a 45-degree angle. In this stance, you are also balanced, but when you move,

the first move should be made by the front foot. For both men and women the knees should be bent slightly for balance.

Hands. Down by your side so that you are free to gesture as you speak. If you are speaking behind a podium, then rest your hands lightly on the top, but do not lean.

Rhythm. There are so many things you can vary to improve your delivery. We do them all quite naturally in our one-on-one conversations and, chances are, if you are really excited and enthusiastic about your subject, they will happen naturally as you move from point to point. It's a good idea to try to work in some variation when you practice. This is especially helpful for the beginner and will add to your confidence. What can you vary? You can raise your brows, wrinkle your nose, shrug your shoulders, anything that comes naturally to you. You can talk fast or slow, pause or ask a question.

Movement. Find out when you accept the invitation to speak whether you will be using a microphone and, if so, what kind. If it is a neck mike, is the cord long enough to move about? If it is on a stand or attached to the speaker's platform, can it be removed? Arrive beforehand and practice removing the mike if you are unsure.

You'll find it quite effective to walk toward your audience to make a point. Then you might move back to the platform to read a poem or check your next topic. You might then leave the platform again and walk over to the side of the room to ask someone in the audience a question and walk back over and stand beside the platform for awhile instead of behind it.

Cords can be tripped over, so you'll want to practice moving about with one. You can attach an extension cord to a cup or other object for this purpose.

Audience. Try to find opportunities to involve the audience, though it is not always possible with every topic or subject. If you are giving a talk on *persuasion,* you might bring up a lady from the audience to persuade. Then, add two others, one to be her yes response, the other to be her no response. You could have each of them tugging on an arm and pulling her back and forth across the room. When you use your imagination and have fun, so does the audience.

FACE-TO-FACE WITH YOUR MIRROR

Part of your preparation should consist of selecting the right wardrobe. On all but the most formal occasions, you should wear what is considered proper business attire. For men, that means a three-piece dark suit, properly tailored and of good quality material, white long-sleeved shirt and dark tie. Socks should always be the color of the trousers.

Business dress for a woman is a skirt with matching jacket and a soft blouse. All should be of good quality and perfectly tailored. Wear basic pumps, no lighter than the hem of your skirt, with a matching leather handbag.

Your appearance sends out powerful signals well before your speech begins. Rules are just rules and, of course, can be varied and broken. The important thing to remember is to dress in a way that will add to your authority and not detract from your message.

Try to stick to the rules until you find a comfort level in public speaking. You will have plenty of time to develop your own style. It is not necessary to blow the budget on your wardrobe in order to be well dressed. Labels are not important, but if you will spend enough money to get a suit of good quality, it will enhance your image and prove quite economical. You can expect years of good service. This type of outfit does not go out of style quickly. Something this basic can be worn again and again, even with the same audience, when varied slightly with a tie, blouse or other accessories.

Don't try to match the dress of your audience. If you are speaking to a group at a local resort, your audience may be in golf or tennis outfits. You came to work. Dress accordingly.

About Face

Okay, after you've prepared your speech and obtained your wardrobe, what do you do? How do you get that first speaking engagement? That's the easy part. There are local civic clubs and church groups that are starving for speakers. Program chairmen are walking around disguised as dentists, secretaries, salespeople. Begin sharing your expertise on your issue with friends and the opportunities will come. Most people want to feel that they are informed, even if they don't do anything.

If you've joined an organization that deals with your issue or issues, you can begin by volunteering your services to their speakers' bureau. If none of the organizations listed in the appendices of this book has a local branch in your area, contact the one that interests you the most and ask about starting one. Then you'll have more than enough opportunities to speak.

God doesn't waste anything. The opportunities are there. All you must do is recognize them and be available.

13

YOU MEAN I'M NEWS?

News is a commodity, a product to be acquired by newspapers, radio and TV stations, which in turn is sold to the public. Where does it come from? It can't be grown like corn or wheat. It can't be manufactured like tires or bathtubs. It can't be purchased like stocks or bonds. Where does it come from? It comes from people like you and me.

There are days when editors opening the morning mail desperately hope for a press release or two worthy of newsprint or air time. They pace nervously into the room with the police radios, and there's nothing but static. They scan the wire machines hoping for a story with a local angle. What they wouldn't give for someone on the phone with an idea for a feature story!

Then there are those days when so much is happening, they can't possibly cover it all. All the crews are on overtime and a story that would normally be a page one headline is reduced to a column on the other side of the comics. On the TV side, it would be down to 20 seconds after the weather.

What Is News?

News comes in two varieties:

Hard news—something that has just happened, is happening right now or will happen in the next few hours. Hard news is aired immediately and headlined in the next edition of the paper.

Feature stories—can be gathered and used within a certain period of time. A feature often involves someone or something unusual, a topic that grips the heart or pocketbook, a story that people never get tired of seeing or a subject that everyone wants to learn more about.

Every organization needs a publicity chairman to work with the local media to further its goals and objectives and get its news to the public. One person, and one person only, should handle the job of publicity. More than one is confusing to the media. That person must be someone who will get to know these media contacts on a one-to-one basis, learn what is expected and needed from each one, and be ready to provide it. The publicity person will also provide access to others in his or her group who can speak with authority on local issues. This provides a local angle when a comment is needed on a national story. The publicity person is responsible for alerting the media to group functions that will be of interest to the public and for providing interview opportunities with national figures who may come into town to address the group for a banquet or other event.

Identify Your Contacts

A publicity chairman is a lot like a produce salesman.

When news is plentiful, you can't give your story away. When it's not, it's valuable merchandise. You must recognize that timing, as well as effort, may determine the amount of newsprint or air time you receive. Like any good salesman, the first thing you must do is get to know the territory and identify those people who can market your product.

As you make your contacts, keep in mind that you are there to provide a valuable service. You should not go in with your hat in your hand to beg for coverage. Keep in mind, however, that the best people in any profession have servant hearts and spirits.

Know Your Media

Newspapers

The small town weekly—Even if you live in a large city, it is often made up of communities that have weekly newspapers which fit into this category. If this is the case, it may take some time to establish a relationship with all the community papers in the areas that surround your city. Never underestimate the value of this type of paper. Its readers are extremely loyal, and it is often read more thoroughly than the large metropolitan paper. If you live in a small town, you may already know the editor. He or she may go to your church or may live in your neighborhood.

The next step is to establish a business relationship. Write a letter to introduce your club or organization. Follow up with a phone call to schedule an official appointment at the editor's office. Don't call on a Monday or a Tuesday. These are generally deadline days for weekly newspapers that come out on Thursday or Friday. Deadline days are to be avoided at all costs. The only exception is when you have a fast-breaking story: your group has just won a highly publicized court battle, your president has resigned suddenly, and so on.

Small to medium daily—The key person here is called the city editor, metropolitan or metro editor. He or she may pass you on to a person who would most likely handle your club or group—the person in charge of news about religion, women's affairs, politics, men's clubs, education, etc. The introduction will insure that you get the proper attention from the person you are asked to see. Don't try to contact a reporter yourself because they're often moved from subject to subject.

Make an effort to get to know the person in charge of editorials or the letters-to-the-editor column. A good relationship could lead to your being asked to write a letter specifically addressing some issue or problem in the community from time to time. Be aware of deadlines when you attempt to contact these people. A morning paper's first edition deadline is late afternoon. Folks who work for an afternoon paper are busiest in the early mornings.

Large daily—Make at least one attempt to reach the city editor, but do not be disappointed or feel rejected if you are put off. Large dailies have editors for practically everything, so go directly to the editor who is likely to have the most interest in your group. This editor may suggest that you see another or may personally provide an introduction. Try to make contact with someone in the editorial department and have your organization cross-referenced in their editorial telephone files.

News Services

When you read your local newspaper, often you will notice that the letters AP or UPI follow the name of the city at the beginning of the story. These are the initials of the two major wire service bureaus, Associated Press and United Press International. When you see those letters at the beginning, it means that the newspaper did not have one of its reporters cover the story, but got the material from one of these large news gathering organizations. The wire services have bureaus in most major cities in the world and have individuals known as stringers or correspondents in many of the smaller ones, as well. They will be interested in hearing from you because they send out a schedule of the day's events by time and give local contacts.

Check your phone directory, and if a wire service is listed, write a short introductory letter. Tell them about your organization and offer to serve as a source whenever one of the issues your organization has taken a stand on is in the news. Attempt to follow up by phone. That's the only way to contact a wire service. These folks are usually overworked, so don't take it personally if they seem abrupt. The wire services have the ability to get your message out to almost every newspaper, TV and radio station in the country immediately. Put them at the top of your list for your press releases and media events.

Many large cities have a news-gathering organization known as City News Service (CNS). CNS handles news of that city and the surrounding metropolitan area. Their reports are sent on Teletype machines much like Associated Press and United Press International. Many small papers and radio stations rely heavily on this service. CNS will be happy to include your events on their schedule.

Radio

Make contact with the news director at each radio station in your area. Many stations are automated and have few local newscasts. These are usually short and of what is called in the trade the "rip and read" variety, right off the UPI and AP Teletype machines. You should have no trouble reaching the news director by phone, but be aware of his or her limitations. They are usually interested only in very important stories that are happening at the moment and can do little more than give headlines.

Know something about each radio station before you call. Most good-sized cities now have at least one *all-talk* station. The news director at one of these stations should be very happy to hear from you. They have the time and welcome the opportunity to air many different views, particularly if they are controversial.

Offer to have your organization's local leader or any of the other local experts in your organization call in for a comment when one of your issues is in the news. Contact the producer, not the personality, of any phone-in talk shows on the station. Send them regular information on your organization and offer to make your local and national experts available. Check with each station's program director for any public service programming that might utilize your group. Ask for guidelines on obtaining public service spots to make announcements on upcoming meetings, activities and programs of your group.

Television

The assignment editor is the person you want to get to know in the television newsroom. Make sure your number is on file and cross-referenced on his or her desk so that you can make your experts available when the station needs a local comment on a national story.

When you contact a TV assignment editor with a story idea, make sure it has visual impact. Simple one-on-one interviews are no-nos on a TV news show. That simply means a TV station will not consider doing an interview unless there is something else to film. Television stations will come out for marches, picket lines, prayer vigils or anything else that is visual. They will do one-on-one interviews at these events and then intercut them with other action footage.

It is bad form to call anyone in a television newsroom in late afternoon. Everyone is involved in last-minute show preparations. It also is considered impolite to call during the news show itself. You are supposed to be watching it.

You should contact the public service director at each of the local television stations as well. After your introductory letter, make an appointment to meet this person. Stations make spot announcements available to nonprofit groups in different lengths—10, 20, 30 and 60 seconds. These are run like commercials, usually in the off hours. Off hours on a TV station can translate into thousands of people. The public service director will be happy to give you guidelines.

There are many nonprofit groups competing for these spots, so be prepared to give a convincing presentation on the merits of your organization. The station may air a community service program where local issues often are discussed. The public service director can give you the name of the producer and perhaps make the introduction.

At each station, contact the person who prepares the editorials and offer to share new information on your issues. Stations must offer equal time for conflicting viewpoints. Check those guidelines and make use of this time with the best speakers in your organization.

Review your local TV guide for other programs that could use the expert speakers in your organization. Make contact with each show producer, not the host of the program. These producers will be particularly interested when you have nationally known speakers in town for special events.

Don't forget your local educational station. If the station does not produce a newscast, then write to the program director. Check the yellow pages for any cable networks that have broadcast facilities or bureaus in your area.

You can save yourself some time by contacting Public Relations Plus in New Milford, Connecticut. This organization publishes annuals for radio and television, listing all known programs that use guests and other publicity material. These annuals include information on public affairs programing, education, college and cable outlets. The address is P.O. Box 1197, New Milford, Connecticut, 06776; phone: (203) 354-9361.

Magazines

Some cities have their own magazines, such as *Philadelphia, Atlanta, Los Angeles* and *Palm Springs*. There may be other local or regional magazines in your area that might be happy to hear from you. *Bacon's Publicity Checker,* published by R.H. Bacon, 332 S. Michigan Avenue, Chicago, 60604, has a complete list of magazines by category. You can call toll free about ordering a copy at (800) 621-0561. One well-placed story in a magazine can do a lot toward furthering your organization's goals and objectives.

Magazines require a lot of lead-time and many people simply do not have the patience to suggest story ideas and follow them through. One approach you might try is to interest a free-lance writer in exploring an issue from your point of view. You can obtain the names of nonfiction free-lance writers that regularly contribute to magazines from the American Society of Journalists and Authors, 1501 Broadway, Suite 1907, New York, 10036. You should check with your organization's headquarters before attempting to interest a national magazine in a feature story.

Follow Correct Procedure

The Introduction

Your first contact with any of the people we have just discussed should be a short letter of introduction. It should be typed on stationery with your organization's letterhead. Make it conversational and direct. Simply state that you are writing to introduce yourself as the authorized local press representative of a particular organization. Give a little background information on the organization. Mention the things that you feel are really important and that will command respect. If it is a large organization, state the size. List the issues you monitor and promote, and some of your organization's accomplishments. Say that you will be delivering a press kit in a few days, but that you will call first for an appointment. Be sure to keep a copy of your letter in case the first one is lost or misplaced.

When you are preparing for your appointments, remember that you are representing the organization. Nothing but the best will do. First impressions are extremely important. Each editor you visit very likely will think of your organization as you represented it in that first encounter. Wear proper business attire as discussed in chapter 12, and carry your press kits in a briefcase. Take along a pad for making notes.

Your national office should be able to provide you with basic press kit information. You must prepare and include a glossy 8″ × 10″ black-and-white photograph of the local president or chief executive of the organization, along with a biographical sketch. Do the same for any other experts in your organization who are capable and willing to speak for the group.

Arrive early. Remember that editors are very busy people, so be careful not to overextend your visit. Deliver your press kit and take notes on deadlines, types of information desired and any special requirements they may have for press releases. Ask for suggestions on how you might be of service and be sure to leave a number(s) where they can contact you at any hour of the day or night. News does not always happen between nine and five, nor is it prepared between those hours. Someone might have a question about your organization while working on a story for the eleven o'clock news. A press representative must be willing to get up at two in the morning to find a picture or answer questions when necessary. You want the people in the media to know that they can depend on you, no matter what.

The Press Release

The press release is your basic means of communicating with newspapers, radio and television. The only exception is a phone call for a last-minute development of major importance. Even if you are holding a press conference for a specific purpose, you should prepare a release to hand to the press in attendance that will tell them what they've just seen and heard.

Press people are under pressure, always facing the next deadline. It's impossible to grasp everything they are told at one time. That's why it is so important to have all the facts in writing so that they can refer to them again and again, if necessary. At a press conference, you should have a biographical sketch and picture for each person that is featured. No matter how famous the person, don't assume the reporter covering the story will know that person.

Press releases make up a good portion of the mail delivered to newspapers, radio and TV stations. The editor or reporter opening the stack on his or her desk will probably spend just a few seconds scanning each one before deciding whether to put it into a file or toss it in the trash can. If the release is nonstandard, poorly written or the facts are blurry, chances are it will wind up in the trash. These reporters and editors just don't have the time to wade through a poorly done press release to sort out the facts or to correct mistakes. They'll just ignore the story. Make sure your press release is considered by following these rules:

1. Type your release on plain white 8½ × 11" paper. You may use a small logo from your organization at the top, but nothing else. Fancy, tinted news bureau stationery is considered in poor taste by some.

2. Releases should be double spaced for newspapers and magazines, triple spaced for television and radio, all on one side of the page only. Leave wide margins.

3. Your name, address, day and night phone numbers

should be placed in the upper-left corner.

4. Leave at least a two-inch block in the upper right corner for the editor to write a headline and make other notes. Do not write a headline yourself.

5. Type *Immediate Release* flush with the right margin unless there is a good reason for holding it until a certain hour.

6. Be brief, never using more than two pages, one if possible. Stick with the facts. Any editorializing will be viewed as manipulative.

7. Indent for paragraphs. Do not divide paragraphs between pages. Do not break words at the end of a line.

8. Begin with a dateline, which consists of the city (all caps), followed by a comma and the state (upper and lower case letters). Use the traditional abbreviations rather than the two-letter postal abbreviations for states except for Alaska, Hawaii and states with five letters or less which are written out. Use two dashes and then begin copy.

9. The first sentence may be used to create interest, but be sure to answer *who, what, where, when, why* and *how* in the first paragraph. In the second paragraph give more details, list key speaker(s) or issue(s). Quote your president or main speaker in the third paragraph, if appropriate. Follow with necessary background information and end with a paragraph summarizing some important facts about your organization.

10. Use short sentences with active verbs.

11. If release is longer than one page, type *(more)* at the bottom of the first page. Put *2-2-2-2* in the top left corner of the second page. Directly underneath type a one- or two-word identifier.

12. Check spelling, grammar and facts.

13. At the end of the release, skip a line and type *-30-* or ### in the center of the page.

14. Whenever possible, hand-deliver your releases. There is no substitute for personal contact. This allows you to suggest an angle or ask if more information is needed. But be brief—only one release at each publication or station. If you must mail, do it well in advance of the event.

Most newspapers and magazines follow the guidelines in the *Associated Press Stylebook and Libel Manual.* You can order a copy by writing to *Stylebook,* AP Newsfeatures, 50 Rockefeller Plaza, New York, 10020. This manual will answer any questions you may have about using titles, abbreviations, numbers, etc. When you conform to accepted standards, this minimizes the editor's work and makes you and your organization look good.

Press Photos

Pictures help sell newspapers and will call attention to your story. Pictures of babies, animals or pretty girls sell more newspapers and will call even more attention to your story. Use them whenever possible.

Newspapers cannot use snapshots or Polaroid prints. They must have good quality, glossy 8″ × 10″ black-and-white prints. Do you have a professional photographer in your organization who can take the photos? If not, unless you are an extremely good photographer, better hire a professional. Some of the smaller papers you visit may use outside photographers and may be able to suggest someone.

There is a big difference between a professional studio photographer and a professional news photographer. A news photographer knows how to make the picture tell the story or how to create interest by setting up an unusual picture. Avoid pictures of people standing and looking at the camera. Try to create some action and don't use more than two or three people in a photograph, if at all possible. Take a good look at what's in the background. Avoid anything that looks busy, such as flowered wallpaper. Ask yourself, "Is there a tree or another object that looks as if it is growing out of the subject's head?"

Look for an unusual setting. Put a couple of people in a dumpster to kick off a clean-up campaign. Put your new president on top of a roof or on top of a hill to signify he or she reached the top.

The larger papers will want to use their own photographers, so if you are setting up an unusual picture, let these papers know in advance so they can send their own people. Ask yourself if it's something television could use as well.

Always provide a full and factual caption for each picture. Identify all people in the photo from left to right. This can be typed and taped on the back of the picture. Never write or type directly onto the back of a photograph. If you are sending out a lot of pictures, there are companies in most large cities that duplicate press photos and print the caption right on the bottom of the picture.

The Follow-through

Resist the temptation to call an editor to ask if he or she received your press release and is going to use it. This is unprofessional. You will see the release if it comes out in the paper. Don't ask editors to send copies of the stories or tapes of programs. If an editor should send you a copy, write a thank-you note immediately.

Always be on the lookout for feature story possibilities. Everyone loves a good feature. Give your feature idea to only one person at a time. Give that person ample time to respond, and make sure he or she is not going to use it before giving it to someone else. Spread these ideas around from one newspaper or television station to another. Most people want to learn more about the issues that face them. The feature writer's biggest problem is the same as that of the news reporter—the next deadline. If you can give that person enough background material, including articles from other publications and a list of well-documented facts, that could be enough to pique his or her interest. One feature possibility would be a story on the campaign generated to pass or defeat an issue.

Don't beg for coverage or ask for favors. If your stories aren't getting printed, then you need to ask yourself, Why not? Simply speaking out at a local school board meeting won't get press coverage, but if you have 25 people outside with protest signs before you speak out, and if you have alerted the media, you should get some action and an interview or two. Having a meeting will not get press coverage, but if you announce the results of a study, give an award, hold a contest, create an unusual display or tie it into a holiday celebration, it might be considered newsworthy.

Timing is more than luck. There is no way to know

when an earthquake, fire or flood may occur, but you should be aware of other major events that are taking place in your city; you also need to know the limitations of your local media. What are the best days for getting maximum news coverage in your city? Be sure to ask the editors when you meet them. The size of the daily newspaper is not determined by the amount of news, but by the amount of advertising in the paper. Your daily paper is largest when the food section comes out. That's the day all the grocery chains place their advertising. If that occurs on Thursday, then have your event on Wednesday.

Time of day also can be important. If you want to make the evening paper, have your event at eight in the morning. Later in the day is fine for a morning paper; it will be reported the following day. Then again, if your event is held too late in the day, you'll blow your chance for coverage on the six o'clock television newscast.

If you decide to hold a press conference, invite everyone. Try to accommodate all those who need one-on-one interviews. There are very few reasons for not granting these requests. If your visiting personality has a plane to catch immediately after a meeting, anticipate this and ask those who may need a personal interview to come a little early.

Never ask a reporter to suppress or kill a story. This is an insult. It seldom works and will make you and your group look bad. Always be truthful. If you find that you have given out some information that is untrue or incomplete, call and correct it as soon as you discover your mistake.

Do not worry about the position the paper or television station has taken on one of your issues in the past. The reporter is an individual. He or she may have a completely different stand, but that is not important. Your goal is simply to have that reporter report your viewpoint or story clearly and factually.

Give everyone good service. It doesn't matter if a reporter is from a tiny weekly paper or one of the industry giants. The reporter from the small weekly paper may be hired by the large daily paper next month or next year. Try to anticipate the special needs and deadlines of each.

Your job is to make the media's job of news gathering easier. Anticipate questions. Always be ready to provide background material to bring a reporter up-to-date on an issue, event or a personality. Reporters have to cover so many different stories in such a short amount of time they may have no knowledge of your subject or the leeway to research it further. So much the better. It is your chance to educate. Never make reporters feel dumb or stupid. They have their jobs because of their ability to size up a situation in a hurry and report the facts. See that they have all the information they need to look good, and they will see that your organization is treated fairly.

14
YOU WANT TO INTERVIEW ME?

As I look back over all the interviews I've done in more than 17 years of broadcasting, a few stand out in my mind. One of the most difficult, but ultimately the most rewarding, was with Mrs. Paul "Bear" Bryant.

In 1972, I got a call from Ed Friedman, the sports producer at *CBS Morning News,* to do a story on the wife of the country's "winningest" big-time college football coach just before the Orange Bowl. It seemed like just another routine assignment.

Mrs. Bryant was the nation's premier football "widow," having spent every Christmas holiday of her married life as part of some bowl-game celebration. Her home away from home at that special time of year was a hotel room, not far from a football field where "The Bear" and his Alabama team prepared to wreak havoc on yet another opponent as their just reward for a winning season.

A perfectly good story. There was one little problem, however. Mary Harmon Bryant was charming and gracious, but very private. She had never done a television interview. She had no desire for the spotlight. She was Paul Bryant's Rock of Gibraltar, but preferred to remain in the background while he basked in the glory of his many gridiron accomplishments. When she finally consented to our interview, I was thrilled!

By the time interview day rolled around, Mary Harmon was a bundle of nerves. She opened the door to her hotel suite that morning in a state of panic, the likes of which I had never seen. I did my best to put her at ease and even helped her put on her make-up.

Friedman sensed the seriousness of the situation and had the crew put as much of the television paraphernalia as possible out of sight. I vaguely remember someone kicking the slate—a fancy chalkboard used to mark scenes to get the audio and video to match in editing—under the couch. We brought in coffee and kicked our shoes off, all of us, and, after what seemed like hours and thousands of feet of film, Mary Harmon relaxed. She forgot about the camera, the crew, the audience, and she just talked to me. Naturally warm and sincere, she stole my heart, the hearts of my crew and, ultimately, the hearts of our viewers.

WINNING THE AUDIENCE

That's really all there is to winning an audience and coming out on top in any interview situation. Just relax, be yourself, forget about the audience and the camera, and talk to the interviewer.

Easier said than done, particularly when you are discussing a controversial topic. I've seen the mere presence of a television camera and a reporter do strange things to people. I've seen them turn a confident, robust man into a scared child who could hardly utter a word, and an otherwise *together* woman into a babbling spring going nowhere.

Dispelling the Fears

Let's take an honest look at the most common fears.

Will I look stupid?

Not if you've done your homework. When you're about to be interviewed it's important that you have more than a working knowledge of your subject. You must practice articulating your views in short, manageable bites. If you're being interviewed for the news, recognize that when your interview is aired, it will run about a minute and a half, two minutes tops.

Ideally the reporter is looking for three good answers, about 20 seconds each, two good 35-second answers will do. If your answer is longer, it probably will be cut. If it is shorter, the editor may string two or three answers together. You don't want that to happen, so practice giving 20-second answers. After awhile it will be easy; you'll have a feel for about how much you can say in 20 seconds.

If you're being interviewed on a talk show or panel discussion, you can go as long as a minute. But if you go much longer, you will start to lose your audience, and the host or moderator will get uneasy and attempt to cut you off.

Will the reporter ask me trick questions and try to back me into a corner?

There really is no such thing as a trick question. If the other side has some convincing arguments, expect to answer those arguments. Don't be fooled or misled or lulled to sleep by the demeanor of the reporter before the interview. The reporter may be the nicest person in the world; the reporter may be on your side; but the reporter must ask you the four or five toughest questions he or she can muster. Expect them. Prepare for them.

Role-play. Pretend you are the reporter. What are the 10 best, most probing questions you could ask someone on that issue. Answer those questions for yourself, over and over, if necessary. Hope you are asked those tough questions. That is the best way to score points with your audience.

It's important to recognize that you will know a lot more about your subject than the reporter. You may have a chance to guide the reporter in what questions to ask before the interview. If you have the chance, give the reporter the arguments for the other side and invite those adversarial questions.

When going over your preparation, don't forget the obvious philosophical questions, such as, "Why is this issue so important to you?" After working so hard to be on top of the latest facts and figures, that's the kind of thing that can throw you if you haven't thought about it. It helps to have someone else make up the questions so that you can practice thinking on your feet.

What if the reporter asks me a question I can't answer?

Don't try to be a know-it-all. I've never met anyone who knows all the answers, have you? Experts often have to call for facts and figures or other pertinent information that may have slipped their minds. It's perfectly normal. If you don't know, say so and offer to get the information for the reporter. If it's important to the story, he or she will stop the tape while you dig it out or make a phone call. If the reporter wants to continue, you can call with the information later and he or she can write it into the show script. Just tell the reporter you want to make sure he or she has the current information. The reporter will appreciate that.

The absolute worst thing you can do is fake it. If you try to pretend that you know the answer and wander all around the subject, it will become clear that you don't know. Even worse, it may look as if you're trying to hide something. You can be sure that part will wind up on the evening news. Have you ever seen an "I don't know, but let me get that information for you" on the news? No, you haven't, but it's done all the time. It's perfectly normal. It's noncontroversial. It's not worth air time, so it's edited out.

If the question that was asked was on a totally different subject, just say, "That's not my area of expertise." You might offer to introduce them to someone who specializes in that issue or subject if you can. Don't be tempted to charge off into an unfamiliar field or issue.

Hypothetical questions also are dangerous and unnecessary. You are perfectly justified in saying something like, "That's a hypothetical question and any answer I could give really wouldn't be meaningful. I'll be happy to answer any of your questions directly relating to this issue." Be polite but firm.

Never, never say, "No comment." A good reporter will not let that go, and it sets up a confrontation.

What if I know the answer but I don't want to answer the question?

Don't attempt to evade a question. This, too, could set

up an unnecessary confrontation. For very good reasons, there will be some questions that you simply won't answer. It is always best to say so and state your case. Say you're sorry but you cannot answer that question because it's a personal matter and you have that understanding with your family, or you can't discuss that issue until it's settled in the courts, or it's an organizational trade secret. Does Macy's tell Gimbel's?

Do answer all legitimate questions on the subject or issue the reporter has come to discuss. If you or your organization has made a mistake, admit it and go on to a more positive topic. "Yes, we blew it, but we learned from that experience and here are the positive results." Everyone makes mistakes and almost anyone can relate to an answer such as this.

Don't feel obligated to do more than answer the question that was asked. Sometimes a reporter will wait, hoping that you will feel uncomfortable with the silence and blurt out more information. It's the reporter's job to fill the silence or edit it out. You just sit there and smile comfortably.

What if I need more time to come up with the answer?

There are some legitimate ways to stall. Sometimes it is quite helpful to have a few more seconds to formulate your answer before you begin to speak. If the question is long and complicated, don't hesitate to ask that it be repeated or explained more fully. You can give yourself a few more seconds by repeating the question yourself before you answer. You can put in a meaningless phrase like, "I'm glad you asked that question" or "That brings up an interesting point." Be sure to pause before you begin your answer so that the editor can extract the excess baggage. Often a simple pause is all you really need to get your thoughts together. Don't be afraid to take that pause to collect your thoughts or just to breathe.

What if the reporter doesn't ask the questions that will allow me to make the points I feel are important?

You can't wait for the right questions; they may never come. As part of your preparation, decide on the one or two main points that you feel are really important and practice working them into the interview. Answer any question thrown at you, and then turn that answer into a springboard for making your point. You'll get good at it with practice. It should be done as soon as possible, for you have no way of knowing how long the interview may last. The way to make sure the point you want to make is the one that winds up on the tube is to make it colorful, quotable or controversial.

What if I make a mistake or bobble during the interview?

Accept the fact that you're going to make mistakes and don't worry about them. After watching anchorpeople go through their paces night after night, it's no wonder we get the idea that we are expected to answer perfectly all those questions tossed at us. After all, Dan Rather can deliver an endless stream of words without missing a beat. Yes, he can, but the words are projected on a glass right in front of the camera lens. Dan Rather, in an interview situation, would be just like the rest of us. He would make a mistake occasionally, correct himself when necessary and go right on. We do that all the time in normal conversation.

If you find that you've given the wrong information, by

all means correct yourself. If you've gotten your words so mixed up that you can't get out of it gracefully, just say, "I'm going to try that again." Pause so the editor can cut out the bad part and start your answer again. If you're on live, just say, "Let me get my tongue untied and I'll try that again." It shows you're human, and as long as you don't get flustered or embarrassed, the audience will be with you.

Have you noticed the reporter's questions are always perfectly delivered? That's because, after the interview, the camera is then focused on the reporter who asks those same questions all over again. He keeps at it until they are perfect. That's show biz! The reporter's goofs often are saved by the crew and presented en masse at staff parties where he is openly ridiculed.

ELIMINATING SELF-CONSCIOUSNESS

Those are the common concerns that sometimes paralyze people before their first media encounter. When you examine them and do your homework, there really is nothing to fear. The experience can and should be quite enjoyable. There is a lot of paraphernalia and excess baggage that goes along with a television interview that can be distracting—the lights, the camera, the cables, the crew. Take a good look at all of that when you first arrive or when they first arrive, then forget it and forget the crew until after the interview. It may help you to know that the crew members are so busy doing their job, they probably will not listen to what you are saying. The camera person is concerned about focus, the lighting person with shadows and the audio person with sound—not the words, just the quality of the sound.

Concentrate on the reporter and the reporter alone. Look at the reporter, maintain good eye contact, talk to the reporter. Your goal is to educate that one person. Think of nothing else. This will go a long way toward eliminating any self-consciousness because you are not thinking about self or the ultimate audience. The audience is not there. For your purpose, it does not exist.

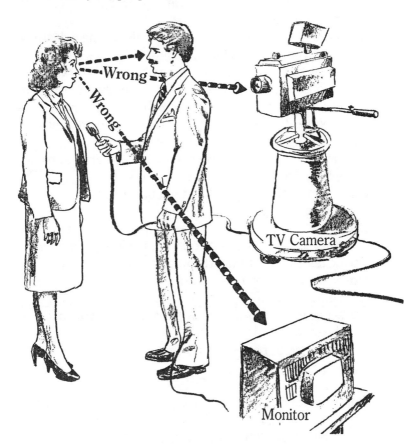

DO'S AND DON'TS THAT WILL SERVE YOU WELL

DO'S

Do make a friend of the reporter. This is a person with feelings just like yours. It's not important whether the reporter is on your side of the issue, only that he or she treats you fairly. The reporter may be on your side by the time the interview is over if you've done your job well.

Do smile at all times, unless you are discussing a death or an extremely sad situation. Remember the old saying, "Smile and the world smiles with you." You want the audience to be with you. It is especially important to smile if the interviewer seems hostile. It's hard for a reporter to work up a confrontation if you're smiling.

Do be warm, friendly and conversational.

Do call the host or interviewer by his or her first name, even if he or she calls you Mr. or Mrs.

Do give quotable, colorful statements.

Do add humor whenever possible.

Do remember that the reporter represents the public, so consider the questions from the public's point of view.

Do be honest and straightforward at all times.

Do be positive in your answers.

Do be concise.

Do act as if you are on-the-air from the time you arrive at the studio.

Do take time to pause, breathe and enjoy.

DON'TS

Don't fill your pauses with extraneous sounds like "er," "uh" and "well, uh."

Don't try to dazzle with fancy vocal footwork.

Don't get into a shouting match with a reporter. Be courteous at all times.

Don't try to run off with the interview. It's the reporter's show.

Don't feel obliged to accept a reporter's facts and figures.

Don't say anything off the record. Anything you say can and will be used.

Don't repeat a reporter's buzz words unless they suit your purpose.

Don't use in-house terminology.

Don't ever lie to a reporter.

Don't let a reporter cut you off before you have finished. If this happens, simply pause and finish your answer. If this happens too many times, there may be a reason. Shorten your answers.

Don't waste a reporter's time.

Don't get flustered if you are asked several questions at once. Say, "You've asked several very good questions. I'll answer the most important one first."

Don't assume you are off-camera at any time before, during or after the interview.

Don't be caught with a grumpy or disinterested look on your face.

Put Your Best Foot Forward

When you are being interviewed on television, you are representing not only yourself and your organization, but in a much larger sense, everyone who shares your views. You'll want to do everything possible to look your best.

Most people, when confronted with their television image for the first time, say, "Do I really look like that?" Many times the answer is "No, you don't really look like

Right

Wrong

that." Television can be unkind if you don't know the tricks of the trade.

Dress. Proper business attire is a must. Everything in chapter 12 applies here, but there are some additional factors you need to keep in mind. Wear solid colors in the dark to middle range. Avoid white; it glares. Black is equally as bad. As the camera adjusts for these colors, your skin color is washed out. Patterns, checks and plaids can make you look like the fat man or fat woman at the circus. Don't wear heavy jewelry that can catch the light and draw attention to itself. You want the audience to be focused on you and what you have to say.

Men, wear a light blue or beige shirt. Avoid pin stripes. Some will appear to "dance" or move back and forth on camera.

Women, avoid any material that rustles. This drives audio people crazy and they will drive you crazy trying to solve their microphone problems. Avoid lots of ruffles, plunging necklines, anything that might cause you to be self-conscious or detract from your authority.

Eyeglasses. Leave them off if you can manage without them. If not, avoid the photosensitive type. The television lights will cause these lenses to go dark and they will make you look as if you are trying to hide. If you're going to be doing a lot of television, you may want to invest in a pair with special glass developed to reduce reflection.

Hair. Keep it attractively styled and simple. Make sure it is well back from the face. Hair can cause unflattering shadows. If you wear your hair swept forward or in bangs, make sure it is well out of the eyes. Hair that is anywhere near your eyes seems to grow on camera and also can make you appear as if you are hiding.

Facial hair. Men, if you wear a mustache, keep it small

Wrong

Right

How to Shape Brows

The Gloom and Doom

The Blah Stare   The Surprise

and well trimmed. If your mustache is too long, the audience will wonder where the sound is coming from if they can't see your lips move. If you have a beard, it must be well trimmed. Check it carefully. Beards also seem to grow on television.

Make-up. This is a necessity for both women and men under the hot lights. Most people look completely washed out without it. If you're going to the television studio, a make-up artist will be provided at stations where it is a union requirement. In nonunion stations, newscasters and reporters are on their own, and so are you.

Don't you chance going on without it. Guys, go to your local drug store—send your wife or sister if you're embarrassed—and buy a small cake of pancake make-up, slightly darker than your skin. It applies easily with a damp sponge. You can carry it with you and dash into the men's room to put it on just before you go on the air or before the film crew arrives.

Gals, you too may want to invest in some pancake make-up. A matte finish is highly desirable under the lights. Try going a little darker than normal with all of your make-up—not heavier, just darker. Avoid pearlized or glittery lipstick and eye shadow. A lesson with a professional make-up artist is always a good investment.

Posture and poise. The way you stand, sit and walk can add to your own confidence and the authority you present to others. The unspoken-message you project with your body is often intensified by the camera.

The most important element of your unspoken-image is your posture. A man should stand with his feet directly under the shoulders, weight evenly distributed between the heels and balls of the feet. A woman would use the pedestal stance. It slims your hips and is more flattering to

Wrong   Right   Right

your legs. To assume the pedestal stance, place one foot slightly in front of the other, back toe turned outward at a 45-degree angle. You should feel comfortable and perfectly balanced.

Try your stance in front of a full-length mirror. Imagine that there is a string attached to the top of your head and you are being pulled upward. Let it pull until your feet can hardly remain on the floor. As you do this, your body should be perfectly aligned. Now bend your knees, ever so slightly, for better balance. Use this basic position whenever you are standing in one spot. Practice moving about and returning to this position. A woman should begin any move with her front foot.

Have you ever examined your walk? Do you move aimlessly from place to place, or do you move with energy and direction? Try walking back and forth with vitality and purpose. Imagine that string pulling on your head until your body is perfectly aligned as you move. Don't lock your knees. Keep them flexed for balance and control. Men should keep their toes pointed straight ahead and on imaginary lines drawn directly under each armpit. It is more flattering for a woman to place one foot directly in front of the other on one imaginary line running through the center of her body. Let your toes turn out slightly and keep your hips pinched tightly together and rolled under. Practice in heels and come down with the weight on the ball of first one foot and then the other.

Now, let's try sitting. Walk to the chair. Turn completely around and feel the chair with the backs of your legs. A woman in the pedestal stance would feel the edge of the chair with her back leg only. Now use the strength in your legs to sit straight down. Don't reach with your fanny. With your hands on the bottom or sides of the chair, slide

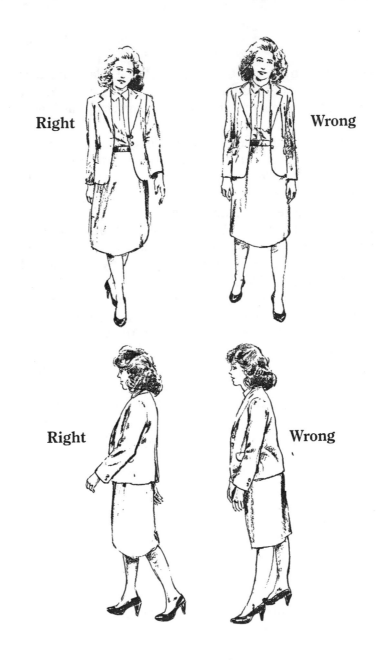

Right

Wrong

Right

Wrong

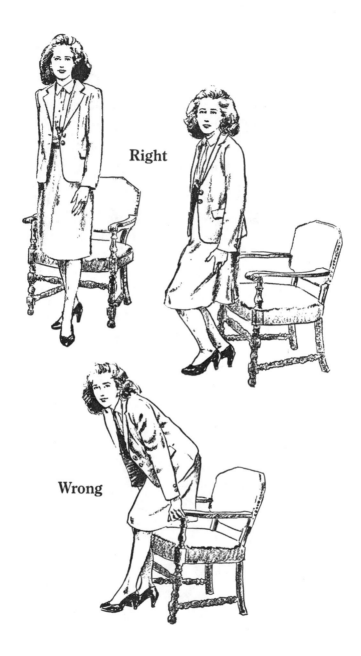

Right

Wrong

Right

Wrong

Wrong

Right

back into a comfortable position.

If you are seated in a swivel chair, which often is the case with any type of panel discussion, resist the temptation to wrap your feet around the base or move back and forth. You'll be safe if you keep your feet planted firmly on the ground. Remember to use good posture and don't slouch just because you're in a chair. You can avoid looking rigid or stiff if you'll sit with your body at a slight angle to the back of the chair. If the chair has arms, rest only one of your arms on the arm of that chair. If you will lean forward ever so slightly, you will appear very interested in the conversation; but be careful—if you lean forward too much, you will appear over eager.

A special word to women. Keep your knees together at all times and, right after you sit, use your hands, in one easy motion, to smooth your skirt down against your legs on each side of your body. Practice doing this in front of a mirror until you are comfortable. Keep your legs in the pedestal stance while seated, or cross them at the ankles and bring them to one side.

As you watch television, you will see every one of these rules broken by some of the tube's biggest stars. This is their medium. They've had a lot of time to discover what works for them on camera and what doesn't. Their make-up, or lack of it, is tested. Wardrobe people often take new clothes to the set and test them on camera before the stars wear them. You don't have that luxury, so play if safe. Don't risk diluting your message!

CONCLUSION

Psalm 11:3 asks a very important question: "When the foundations are being destroyed, what can the righteous do?"

The late Martin Niemoller, a German theologian, was among the survivors of the Holocaust years under Adolph Hitler. A well-known story of that experience is attributed to him. It goes like this:

> *In Germany they came first for the Communists, and I didn't speak up because I wasn't a Communist.*
>
> *Then they came for the Jews, and I didn't speak up because I wasn't a Jew.*
>
> *Then they came for the trade unionists, and I didn't speak up because I wasn't a trade unionist.*
>
> *They they came for the Catholics, and I didn't speak up because I was a Protestant.*

Then they came for me, and by that time no one was left to speak up.[1]

Have you begun to speak up, or are you still getting ready?

What have you done about pornography, abortion, the humanist textbooks in your child's school? What have you done about the sex shops or prostitution in your own neighborhood? What have you done about the clinic in your child's school, set up to dispense birth control devices without your knowledge or consent, to go along with the how-to course in sex taught without moral values down the hall? What have you done about speaking out against the ERA, which may force our government to pay for abortions and send your daughters to war? What have you done to speak out against comparable worth, the wage-setting system that will socialize our economy? What have you done about the lyrics in rock music and the constant doses of violence and sex that invade our homes through the airwaves and cable TV?

The authors of *Vital Signs* published vast amounts of statistical information about those who call themselves Christians in this country. They concluded that there is "no acceptable excuse for Christians not to have revolutionized the world for Jesus' sake." They theorize that many of the Americans who call themselves Christians must be "playing a grand game—playing church."[2]

Perhaps they are right, but I believe a good many of us simply spend all our time getting ready. We are awed by the task because we have failed to break it down into bite-sized pieces. Maybe you are not ready to appear on "Sixty Minutes" or to run for Congress or to be the chairman of a nationwide campaign against pornography. But you can write a letter or make a phone call. God is waiting to use you right where you are. Don't wait until you can devote days or months to some of these problems. God can use 15 minutes.

I am not suggesting that participating in the affairs of your community and government take the place of daily prayer and studying the Word. It must begin with those things. Without a personal knowledge of the Word and a personal relationship with Him, you cannot know when you are being deceived or what is required.

By the grace of God declare yourself *ready* and go to Him. "Whatever makes men good Christians, makes them good citizens."[3]

NOTES

Introduction

1. Paul Kurtz, A Secular Humanist Declaration (Buffalo, NY: Prometheus Books, 1980).
2. Humanist Manifesto I & II (Buffalo, NY: Prometheus Books, 1973).
3. "The Mother of the Women's Liberation Movement," *Kansas City Times*. April 6, 1981.
4. Gloria Steinem, Saturday Review of Education, March 1973.

Chapter 1

1. James Madison. Public domain.
2. Paul Kurtz, *A Secular Humanist Declaration* (Buffalo, NY: Prometheus Books, 1980).
3. Coleen McMurray, "Religion in America," The Gallup Report #236, May 1985.
4. Edmund Burke. Public domain.
5. D. James Kennedy, Address to the American Coalition for Traditional Values, October 15, 1985.
6. Thomas Jefferson. Public domain.

7. D. James Kennedy, Address to the American Coalition.
8. George Barna and William Paul McKay, *Vital Signs* (Westchester, Ill: Crossway Books, 1984), p. 4.
9. Patt Morrison, "AIDS Unit for Youngsters: A Tragic Necessity at L.A. Childrens Hospital," *Los Angeles Times,* July 21, 1986, sec. 1, p. 3, col. 3.
10. Ibid.
11. Paul Houston, "Adult Material: X in Chicago, Ex in Atlanta," *Los Angeles Times,* July 21, 1986, sec. 1, p. 1, col. 3.
12. Stuart Briscoe, *Bound for Joy* (Ventura, CA: Regal Books, 1982).
13. Martin Luther. Public domain.

Chapter 3
1. Doug Esser, "Issue of Decade," *The Register-Guard,* December 16, 1984, p. B-1.
   Kathryn B. Steckert, "Why Aren't You Earning More," *Glamour* (June 1986), p. 275.
2. *Facts on File,* (New York, NY: Facts on File Publications, 1984), p. 517.
3. Speech delivered by Linda Chavez, staff director of the U.S. Commission on Civil Rights, at Concerned Women for America's National Convention in Washington, D.C., September 19, 1986.
4. *Bureau of the Census,* 1985 study.
5. U.S. Bureau of Labor Statistics, Dept. of Labor figure.
6. *Comparable Worth: Issue for the '80s,* A Consultation of the U.S. Commission on Civil Rights, vol. 2: Proceedings of June 6-7, 1984, p. 180.
7. Based on data from U.S. Department of Labor document no. 86-434.
8. Doug Esser, "Job Comparison Cannot Be Made," *The*

Register-Guard, December 16, 1984, p. B-1.
9. Steckert, p. 175.
10. Esser, "Issue of Decade," p. 1.
11. Peter Johnson, "Washington State Reaches Comparable Worth Accord," *USA TODAY,* January 2, 1986, p. A-3.
12. Doug Esser, "Job Comparison Cannot Be Made," p. 2.
13. Study conducted by Mark Killingsworth, Associate Professor of Economics, Rutgers University 1972-1977.
 Linda Chavez, "Pay Equity Is Unfair to Women," *Fortune Magazine,* March 4, 1985, p. 162.
14. *Comparable Worth: An Analysis and Recommendations.* A Report of The United States Commission on Civil Rights, June 1985, p. 70.
15. George Gilder, "Women in the Work Force," *Atlantic Monthly* (September 1986), p. 22.
16. Averages in 1985, as published in *Employment and Earnings,* Bureau of Labor Statistics, U.S. Department of Labor, January 1986.
17. Gilder, p. 22,23.
18. *Employment and Earnings,* p. 191.
19. Gilder, "Women in the Work Force," p. 22.
20. *Comparable Worth: Issue for the 80's,* p. 75.
21. Killingsworth study and Chavez, "Pay Equity Is Unfair to Women."
22. Phyllis Schlafly, "Comparable Worth: Unfair to Men and Women," *The Phyllis Schlafly Report,* vol. 18, no. 12, sec. 1, p. 4.
23. U.S. Dept. of Labor document no. 86-484.
24. *Comparable Worth: An Analysis and Recommendations,* p. 47.

25. Ibid., p. 69.
26. Phyllis Schlafly, "Comparable Worth Is Not Comparable or Worthy," *The Phyllis Schlafly Report,* vol. 20, no. 4, sec. 1, p. 2.
27. National Academy of Sciences study, 1981.
28. U.S. Commission on Civil Rights study, 1984.

Chapter 4
1. Report, Subcommittee on Separation of Powers to Senate Judiciary Committee, S-158, 97th Congress.
2. Kenneth L. Woodward with Mark D. Uehling, "America's Abortion Dilemma," *Newsweek* (January 14, 1985), p. 29.
3. *Ibid.,* p. 28.
4. "Conceived in Liberty," *American Portrait Films,* Anaheim, California, 1984.
5. S. Henshaw, "Competition Cutting into Case Loads," *OB-GYN News* (September 1, 1984).
6. Woodward & Uehling, "America's Abortion Dilemma," p. 26.
7. "Conceived in Liberty."
8. Ann Saltenberger, *Every Woman Has a Right to Know the Dangers of Legal Abortion* (Glassboro, New Jersey: Air-Plus Enterprises, 1983), p. 164.
9. Jamie Murphy, "Abortion's Shrinking Majority," *Time* (June 23, 1986), p. 30.
10. Phil Hager, "High Court Voids Abortion Curbs," *Los Angeles Times,* June 12, 1986, part I, p. 1.
11. Murphy, "Abortion's Shrinking Majority," p. 30.
12. Hager, "High Court Voids Abortion Curbs," p. 1.
13. Woodward, "America's Abortion Dilemma," p. 22.
14. Thomas J. Balch, esq., "*Roe* v. *Wade:* Abortion Is Legal Throughout Pregnancy," *AUL Legal Defense*

Fund, p. 3.

15. Frankie Schaffer, *A Time for Anger* (Westchester, Illinois: Crossway Books, 1982), p. 156.
16. Duenhoelter & Grant, "Complications Following Prostaglandin F-2 Alpha Induced Midtrimester Abortion," *Journal of OB & Gyn* (September 1975).
17. Woodward, "America's Abortion Dilemma," p. 26.
18. "Conceived in Liberty."
19. Woodward, "America's Abortion Dilemma," p. 26.
20. "Conceived in Liberty."
21. Ibid.
22. Bernard N. Nathanson, M.D., *The Abortion Papers: Inside the Abortion Mentality* (New York: Frederick Fell Publishers, Inc., 1983), p. 162.
23. Henshaw, "Competition Cutting into Case Loads."
24. Dr. Micheline Matthews-Roth of the Harvard Medical School on *CBS Morning News,* March 4, 1985.
25. Professor Dan Robinson, a neuropsychologist at Georgetown University Hospital on *CBS Morning News,* March 4, 1985.
26. "Charges Disputed: MD Group Claims That Fetuses Suffer Pain," *American Medical News* (February 24, 1984), p. 15.
27. "Why Pain Hurts: Unlocking an Agonizing Mystery," *Time* (June 11, 1984), p. 61.
28. "Ronald Reagan to National Religious Broadcasters," *New York Times,* January 31, 1984.
29. *American Medical News,* p. 15.
30. Ibid.
31. Elizabeth Mehren, "A Refutation of 'Silent Scream,'" *Los Angeles Times,* August 17, 1985, sec. V, p. 7.
32. Abortion Statistics, United States, 1982-83, pre-released to state health agencies, 1986.

33. Willke, *Abortion Questions & Answers* (Cincinnati, Ohio: Hayes Publishing Co., 1985), p. 185.
34. C. Everett Koop, *The Right to Live the Right to Die* (Wheaton, Illinois: Tyndale House Publishers, Inc., 1980), p. 67.
35. Woodward, "America's Abortion Dilemma," p. 26.
36. Willke, *Abortion Questions & Answers,* p. 299.
37. Koop, *The Right to Live the Right to Die,* p. 62.
38. Willke, *Abortion Questions & Answers,* p. 209.
39. B. Craver, "Morning After Pill Prevents Pregnancy in Victims of Rape," *Family Practice News* (March 1972).
40. C. Everett Koop as told to Dick Bohrer, "Deception on Demand," *Moody Monthly* (May 1980).
41. Koop, "Deception on Demand."
42. "Pro-Life Doctors Speak Out," *Pro-Life Video Library, vol. 1., American Portrait Films, Anaheim, California, 1986.*
43. Koop, "Deception on Demand."
44. "Death on Demand" Pro-Life Video Library, vol. 2, American Portrait Films, Anaheim, California, 1986.
45. S. Harlap et al., "Spontaneous Fetal Losses After Induced Abortions," *New England Journal of Medicine,* vol. 301, pp. 677-681.
46. Nathanson, *The Abortion Papers,* p. 16.
47. "Morbidity and Mortality," U.S. Dept. of Health and Human Services *Weekly Report,* vol. 35, no. 255 (August 1986).
48. Ibid., 1972.
49. Bernard Nathansen, *Aborting America* (Garden City, New Jersey: Doubleday & Co., 1979), p. 193.
50. "Effect of Induced Abortion on Subsequent Reproduction Function," New York State Dept. of Health, Contract # 1-HD-6-2802, 1975-78.

51. "Morbidity and Mortality," U.S. Dept. of Health and Human Services *Weekly Report,* vol. 33, no. 15 (April 20, 1984).

52. Hager, "High Court Voids Abortion Curbs," p. 1.

53. Ibid.

54. Ibid.

55. Charlotte Low, "Whose Right to Choose," *Insight* (January 27, 1987), p. 17.

56. "Morbidity and Mortality," vol. 33, no. 15 (April 20, 1984).

57. Willke, *Abortion Questions and Answers,* p. 104.

58. E. Lenowski, *Heartbeat,* vol. 3, no. 4 (December 1980).

59. Willke, *Abortion Questions & Answers,* p. 137.

60. Minnesota Maternal Mortality Committee, Dept. of OB & GYN, Univ. of Minnesota, *American Journal of OB/GYN,* vol. 6, no. 1 (1967).

61. Dr. Anne C. Speckhard, "Psycho-Social Aspects of Stress Following Abortion," © 1986.

62. J. Kent, R.C. Greenwood, W. Nichols, J. Lochen: "Emotional Sequelae to Therapeutic Abortion," A Comparative Study presented at the meeting of the Canadian Psychiatric Association, 1978.

63. Woodward, "America's Abortion Dilemma," p. 22.

64. Koop, *The Right to Live The Right to Die, p. 61.*

65. *Nathansen, The Abortion Papers,* p. 16.

66. "Birmingham Residents Contest Planned Parenthood Funding," *The Rutherford Institute,* vol. 3, no. 2 (April, May 1986), p. 7.

67. A. Jurs, "Planned Parenthood Advocates Permissive Sex," *Christianity Today* (September 2, 1982); Stan E. Weed, "Curbing Births, Not Pregnancies," *The Wall Street Journal,* October 14, 1986.

68. Marlene Cimons, "Bennett, Koop Settle Aids Dispute," *Los Angeles Times*, January 31, 1987, part I, p. 2.
69. John W. Whitehead, ed., *Arresting Abortion* (Westchester, IL: Crossway Books, 1985), p. 99.
70. "Conceived in Liberty."
71. Barry Siegel, "Fetus: Prenatal Exams Demand Choices," *Los Angeles Times*, November 19, 1986, sec. 1, p. 22.

Chapter 5

1. Ellen Goodman, "It's No Time for Another Full-Fledged ERA Fight," *Los Angeles Times*, November 17, 1986, sec. 2, p. 5.
2. Orrin G. Hatch, *The Equal Rights Amendment—Myths and Realities* (USA: Savant Press, 1983), p. 24.
3. Dr. Donald Joy "The Innate Differences Between Males & Females," *Focus on the Family*, tape CS 099.
4. Ibid.
5. Ibid.
6. Perkins and Silverstein, "The Legality of Homosexual Marriage," *Yale Law Journal* (1982): 573-74.
7. Resolutions of the National Organization for Women, October 1982, Indianapolis, Indiana.
8. Thomas Emerson, "Equal Rights for Women," *The Yale Law Journal*, vol. 80:871.
9. Hatch, *the Equal Rights Amendment*, p. 58.

Chapter 6

1. Alan Sears, "Report on Pornography Commission," Address to Concerned Women for America's Third National Convention, September 1986, tape no. 604.
2. James Dobson, "Combating the Darkness," *Focus on*

the Family (August 1986), p. 2.

3. *Final Report of the Attorney General's Commission on Pornography* (Nashville, TN: Rutledge Hill Press, 1986), p. 298.

4. Ibid., p. 130.

5. Ibid., p. 132.

6. Ibid., p. 138.

7. Ibid., p. 145.

8. Ibid., p. 142.

9. "ACLU Says Child Porn Legal," *National Federation for Decency* (November/December 1986), p. 22.

10. *Final Report,* p. 40.

11. Ibid., p. 42.

12. Sears, tape no. 604.

13. J. Michael McManus, *Introduction to the Final Report of the Attorney General's Commission on Pornography* (Nashville, TN: Rutledge Hill Press, 1986), p. XLVI.

14. Dennis Wharton, "Major Record Companies Agree to Printed Lyrics or 'Explicit' Album Tags," *Variety* (November 3, 1985), p. 1.

15. McManus, *Introduction—Final Report,* p. XLVII.

16. *The Gallup Report,* August 1986, poll no. 251, taken July 1986.

17. *Final Report,* p. 329.

18. Ibid., p. 261.

19. Judith Reisman, "The Porno Industry: Giving Child Molesting Its Stamp of Approval," *The Rutherford Institute,* (January/February, 1986), vol. 3, no. 1, p. 10.

20. "Lifetime Likelihood of Victimization," Bureau of Justice Statistics Technical Report, Document no. NCJ 104274, March 1978.

21. *Final Report,* p. 315-316.

22. Ibid., p. 540.

23. Tim Minnery, ed., *Pornography a Human Tragedy,* (Wheaton, IL: Tyndale House, 1986), pp. 323-29.
24. Ibid., p. 316.
25. *Final Report,* p. 260.
26. Ibid.
27. Minnery, *Pornography a Human Tragedy,* pp. 156-59.
28. *Final Report,* p. 198.
29. Robin Richman, "An Infinity of Jimis," *Life* (October 3, 1969), p. 74.
30. Stewart Powell, "What Entertainers Are Doing to Your Kids," *U.S. News and World Report* (October 28, 1985), p. 46.
31. *The Gallup Report,* July 1986.
32. *Let's Talk Rock* (Arlington, VA: Parents Resource Center, 1986), p. 7.

Chapter 7

1. Stan E. Weed, "Curbing Births, Not Pregnancies," *The Wall Street Journal,* October 14, 1986, p. 36.
2. Kathleen McAuliffe, "AIDS: At the Dawn of Fear," *U.S. News and World Report* (January 12, 1987), p. 60.
3. Beverly Beyette, "Teen Sex-Education Campaign Launched," *Los Angeles Times,* October 17, 1986, sec. 5, p. 1.
4. *Family Planning Perspectives* (March/April 1985), vol. 17, pp. 70-75.
5. *Biblical Principles* (Plymouth, MA: Plymouth Rock Foundation, 1984), p. 240.
6. Ruth Bell, *Changing Bodies, Changing Lives* (New York: Random House, 1980), pp. 97,98.
7. Ibid., p. 94.
8. Ibid., p. 114.
9. Ibid., p. 121.

10. Ibid., p. 121.
11. Ibid., p. 87.
12. Ruth Bell, *Our Bodies, Ourselves* (New York: Simon and Schuster, 1979), p. 42.
13. Tom Morganthau, "Future Shock," *Newsweek* (November 24, 1986), p. 39.
14. McAuliffe, "AIDS: At the Dawn of Fear," p. 69.
15. Weed, "Curbing Births, Not Pregnancies," p. 36.
16. Ibid., p. 36.
17. Joseph R. Peden and Fred R. Glahe, eds., *The American Family and the State* (San Francisco: Pacific Research Institute, 1968), p. 338.
18. Barbara Kantrowitz, "Kids and Contraceptives," *Newsweek* (February 16, 1987), p. 54.
19. Ibid., p. 58.
20. Bill Barol, "Koop and Bennett Agree to Disagree," *Newsweek* (February 16, 1987), p. 64.
21. Marlene Cimons, "Bennett, Koop Settle AIDS Dispute," *Los Angeles Times*, January 31, 1987, sec. 1, p. 2.
22. Beyette, "Teen Sex-Education Campaign Launched," p. 23.
23. Ibid., p. 23.
24. "Annual Report," Center for Population Options, 1985.
25. Michael Schwartz, "Planned Parenthood Sells Lifestyle Not Enlightenment," *Our Sunday Visitor* (March 1, 1987), p. 3.
26. Report of the House Select Committeeon Children, Youth and Families, "Teen Pregnancy: What Is Being Done? A State-by-State Look," December 1985, p. 30.
27. Joy Dryfoos, "School Based Health Clinics: A New Approach to Preventing Adolescent Pregnancy?" *Fam-*

ily Planning Perspectives, vol. 17, no. 2 (March/April 1985), p. 73.

28. Asta M. Kenny, "School-Based Clinics: A National Conference," *Family Planning Perspectives,* vol. 18, no. 1, (January/February 1986), p. 45.

29. Schwartz, "Planned Parenthood Sells Life-style Not Enlightenment," p. 3.

30. Weed, "Curbing Births, Not Pregnancies," p. 36.

31. Barrett Mosbacker, *Teen Pregnancy and School-Based Health Clinics* (Washington, D.C.: Family Research Council, 1986), p. 4.

32. Jacqueline R. Kasun, Ph.D., *The Baltimore School Birth Control Study: A Comment* (Stafford, VA: American Life Education and Research, 1986).

33. Joseph Peden and Fred Glahe, eds., *The American Family and the State,* p. 336.

34. *Family Planning Perspectives* (Sept/Oct, 1980), vol. 12, no. 5, p. 229.

35. Schwartz, "Planned Parenthood Sells Life-style Not Enlightenment," p. 3.

36. Elizabeth B. Connell and Howard J. Tatum, *Sexually Transmitted Diseases:* Diagnosis and Treatment (Durant, OK: Creative Infomatics, Inc., 1985), introduction.

37. Leslie Roberts, "Sex and Cancer," *Science 86* (July/August 1986).

38. Rich C. Bump, "Sexually Transmissible Infectious Agents in Sexually Active Asymptomatic Adolescent Girls," *Pediatrics* (April 1986), vol. 77, no. 4., p. 48.

39. Willis, Judith, "Comparing Contraceptives," U.S. Department of Health and Human Services, FDA 85-1123, May 1985.

Chapter 8
1. Charles Dudley Warner, 1897. Public domain.
2. Wendell Phillips. Public domain.
3. Mary Crowley, *Women Who Win* (Old Tappan, NJ: Revell, 1979), p. 42.

Chapter 9
1. President John F. Kennedy, Inaugural Address, 1961. Public Domain.
2. *Power of People,* 1986 Free Congress Foundation slide presentation.
3. Ibid.
4. Ibid.
5. Ibid.
6. Ibid.
7. Ibid.
8. "Get Out the Vote," *1984 Statement of Vote for Connecticut,* published by state of Connecticut, Secretary of State, Election Divison.
9. *Power of People,* 1986 Free Congress Foundation slide presentation.
10. Ibid.
11. Ibid.
12. *Statistical Abstract of the United States* (1982 figure), published by U.S. Department of Commerce, 1986.
13. Gallup Poll, voter turn-out index, 1984.
14. Figures from American Christian Voice Foundation, based on informal polls taken in churches.
15. Henry Wadsworth Longfellow. Public domain.
16. Survey information compiled by Roper Organization on all polls from September 1974-October 1986.
17. Richard Cizik, ed., *The High Cost of Indifference* (Ventura, CA: Regal Books, 1984). Used by permission.

18. Arbitron (New York: Spring Book, 1986).
19. Ibid.
20. Ibid.
21. Simmons Market Research Bureau, New York, NY, July 1985.
22. *Bristol Herald-Courier,* January 17, 1982, p. A-5.
23. Marta McCave, "NEA Libel Suit Hangs over Teacher," *USA TODAY,* August 30, 1983.
24. "NEA Concedes Defeat in Suzanne Clark Case," *Concerned Women for America Newsletter* (December/ January 1984), p. 1.
25. Ibid.
26. *Stand by Me,* Columbia Pictures, 1986.
27. Will Rogers. Public domain.
28. Larry Frerk, Director of Advertising and Public Relations, A.C. Nielsen Media Research Corporation, February 1986 figures.
29. Ibid.
30. Michael Jackman, *Crown's Book of Political Quotations* (New York, NY: Crown Publishers, Inc., 1982), p. 136.

Chapter 10

1. Our American Government—*What Is It? How Does It Function?* (Washington, DC: U.S. Government Printing Office, 1981), p. 46.
2. Ibid.
3. Michael Jackman, *Crown's Book of Political Quotations* (New York: Crown Publishers, Inc., 1982), p. 62.

Chapter 11

1. Orin G. Hatch, *The Equal Rights Amendment—Myths and Realities* (U.S.A.: Savant Press, 1983), p. 86.

2. Louis Harris Poll, 1984.

Chapter 12
1. Lewis Carroll, *Alice in Wonderland.* Public domain.
2. John Bartlett, *Bartlett's Familiar Quotations,* 15th ed. (Boston: Little, Brown and Company, 1980), p. 746. Attributed.

Conclusion
1. John Bartlett, *Bartlett's Familiar Quotations,* 15th ed. (Boston: Little, Brown and Company, 1980), p. 824.
2. George Barna and William Paul McKay, *Vital Signs* (Westchester, IL: Crossway Books, 1984).
3. Daniel Webster. Public domain.

APPENDIX I

RESOURCE ORGANIZATIONS

On the following pages, you will find lists of two types of resource organizations: (1) *membership organizations* with specific agendas, goals, purposes and programs that invite like-minded people into their ranks to work for a common cause, and (2) *educational organizations* that exist primarily to disseminate information to the public on a variety of concerns, often similar to and related to those of the membership groups.

MEMBERSHIP ORGANIZATIONS

You might want to write to several of the following organizations and ask for information, a sample newsletter and membership information. Carefully study the material you receive. Although several organizations may be listed for each issue, they often differ in philosophy, size, methods and member services. Make an informed choice.

American Coalition for Traditional Values
Suite 850
122 C St., N.W.
Washington, DC 20001
(202) 628-2967

For ministers and lay leaders. ACTV funnels moral action material to pastor-reps in each congressional district aimed at restoring moral and spiritual values to government, schools and media.

American Life League
P.O. Box 490
Stafford, VA 22554
(703) 659-4171

A multi-issue pro-life organization that also seeks to eliminate sex, violence and profanity from radio and TV.

American Victims of Abortion
419 Seventh St., N.W.
Washington, DC 20004
(202) 626-8832

AVA coordinates groups of women who have had abortions nationally and provides those who are willing to share testimonies.

Americans Against Abortion
Box 70
Lindale, TX 75771
(214) 963-8676

A pro-life organization.

Christian Action Council
701 W. Broad St., Suite 405
Falls Church, VA 22046
(703) 237-2100

CAC is a pro-life organization that promotes fundamental biblical values, establishes pregnancy centers and maintains a speakers bureau.

Christian Educators Association International
1410 W. Colorado Blvd.
P.O. Box 50025
Pasadena, CA 91105
(818) 798-1124
For Christian educators in public and private schools. CEAI seeks to encourage Christian educators; offers information for parent-action groups; provides curriculum materials; offers legal advice, counsel and representation to government bodies.

Citizens for Decency Through Law
11000 N. Scottsdale Rd.
Suite 210
Scottsdale, AZ 85254
(602) 483-8787
CDL will assist individuals, organizations or local law enforcement officers with legal research, briefs and prosecution of obscene materials.

Citizens for Educational Freedom
Rosslyn Plaza, Suite 805
1611 N. Kent St.
Arlington, VA 22209
(703) 524-1991
CEF promotes local control of public schools, creates respect for religious and moral values of the parents and children, provides options for released-time religious instruction, and promotes educational vouchers of tax

credits for parents who choose to send children to nongovernment schools.

Citizens for Excellence in Education
Box 3200
Costa Mesa, CA 92628
(714) 546-5931
This division of the National Association of Christian Educators promotes both better education in academic subjects, and moral and spiritual values in public education.

Concerned Women for America
122 C. St., N.W.
Suite 800
Washington, DC 20001
(202) 628-3014
A pro-family, pro-life organization that promotes traditional moral values, religious freedom, a strong national defense and the free enterprise system; trains volunteer lobbyists; provides legal defense involving First Amendment rights. Men are also welcome.

Crusade for Life
1695 Crescent Ave.
Anaheim, CA 92801
(714) 999-1620
An evangelical pro-life organization.

Eagle Forum
P.O. Box 618
Alton, IL 62002
(618) 462-5415

Eagle Forum is a pro-family organization that promotes patriotism, traditional moral values, private enterprise and a strong national defense.

International Women in Leadership
P.O. Box 62603
Virginia Beach, VA 23462
(804) 495-5240
IWL is a network of Christian women leaders who have organized to meet the challenge of bringing Kingdom principles into each sphere of influence.

Methodists for Life
12105 Livingston St.
Wheaton, MD 20902
(301) 942-1627
A pro-life organization for Methodist ministers and lay people that pickets, lobbies and operates a speakers bureau.

Morality in Media, Inc.
475 Riverside Dr.
New York, NY 10115
(212) 870-3222
MIM works to eliminate pornography and operates a clearing house for legal information on obscenity cases.

Mothers at Home
P.O. Box 2228
Merrifield, VA 22116
(703) 352-2292
MAH seeks to improve the morale and image of moth-

ers who choose to stay at home to raise their families, maintains a speakers bureau, conducts research and compiles statistics.

National Association of Christian Educators (NACE)
Box 3200
Costa Mesa, CA 92628-3200
(714) 546-5931

This organization of Christian professional educators in public schools is dedicated to bringing academic excellence and moral and spiritual values to public schools.

National Association of Evangelicals
1430 K St., N.W.
Washington, DC 20005
(202) 628-7911

An organization for churches, ministers and lay leaders, the NAE promotes religious liberty and national righteousness, pro-life, stewardship and natural resources, and the proper roles of church, family and government.

National Coalition Against Pornography
800 Compton Rd.
Suite 9248
Cincinnati, OH 45231
(513) 521-1985

An organization that deals specifically with pornography issues.

National Council for Better Education
1800 Diagonal Rd.
Suite 635
Alexandria, VA 2231

Organized for all Americans, this council promotes reform from traditional perspective, advocates local control and teaches parents how to critique curriculum and textbooks.

National Federation for Decency
P.O. Drawer 2440
Tupelo, MS 38803
(601) 844-5036

National Right to Life Committee, Inc.
419 Seventh St., N.W.
Suite 500
Washington, DC 20004
(202) 626-8800
The central, single-issue, pro-life, educational, lobbying and political organization.

National Teens for Life
419 Seventh St., N.W.
Suite 402
Washington, DC 20004
(202) 626-8800
A pro-life organization for junior high and high school students.

Open Arms
P.O. Box 7188
Federal Way, WA 98003
(206) 839-8919
This pro-life, abortion-related ministry for all women, men and families who are victims of abortion provides a confidential, post-abortion and unplanned pregnancy coun-

seling service; also maintains a speakers bureau.

Parents' Music Resource Center
1500 Arlington Blvd.
Suite 300
Arlington, VA 22209
(703) 527-9466
   Organized to identify and combat sexually explicit and excessively violent rock music lyrics.

Plymouth Rock Foundation
P.O. Box 425
Marlborough, NH
(603) 876-4685
   Disseminates information on our American Christian heritage, government, economics, education.

Presbyterians for Life
P.O. Box 953
Decatur, GA 30031
   A pro-life organization for Presbyterian ministers and lay people.

Pro-Life Action League
616 N. Cicero #210
Chicago, IL 60646
(312) 777-2900
   This pro-life organization maintains placement services and children's services, compiles statistics, organizes demonstrations and picketing, provides counseling, engages in lobbying and conducts seminars.

Renaissance Women
205 Third St., S.E.
Washington, DC 20003
(202) 546-4143
Renaissance Women promotes national defense, the free enterprise system and leadership of women.

Rutherford Institute
P.O. Box 510
Manassas, VA 22110
(703) 491-5411
The institute maintains a legal defense of Christian principles.

Students for America
3509 Haworth Dr.
Suite 200
Raleigh, NC 27609
(919) 782-0213, (919) 787-3285
Coalition of conservative students working for traditional family values, a free enterprise system and a strong national defense.

United States Defense Committee
450 Maple Ave. East
Suite 204
Vienna, VA 22180
(703) 281-5517
Promotes strong national defense.

Women Exploited by Abortion
P.O. Box 123

Antioch, IL 60002
(312) 263-1175, (312) 395-8102
An evangelical organization for abortion victims; provides counseling.

EDUCATIONAL ORGANIZATIONS

This group of organizations exists primarily for the purpose of educating the public on some of the issues covered in this book. They can provide invaluable research material if you'll take the time to write for catalogs.

American Security Council
499 S. Capitol St., S.W.
Suite 500
Washington, DC 20003
Provides material on national security issues and defense.

Biblical News Service
P.O. Box 10428
Costa Mesa, CA 92627
(714) 850-0349
Materials offered include Presidential Biblical Scoreboard, Candidate Biblical Scoreboard and Family Protection Scoreboard.

Free Congress Foundation
721 Second St., N.E.
Washington, DC 20002
(202) 546-3004
The foundation is divided into four major programs: The Institute for Government and Politics; the Child and

Family Protection Institute; The American Education Coalition and the Catholic Center for Free Enterprise; and Strong Defense and Traditional Values.

Heritage Foundation
214 Massachusetts Ave., N.E.
Washington, DC 20002
(202) 546-4400
    The foundation advocates free enterprise, limited government, individual liberty and a strong national defense.

International Life Services, Inc.
2606½ W. Eighth St.
Los Angeles, CA 90057
(213) 382-2156
    This organization publishes the Biennial Pro-Life Resource Manual, which includes a complete listing of all pro-life groups in the United States.

Restore a More Benevolent Order Coalition
P.O. Box 10428
Costa Mesa, CA 92627
(714) 850-0349
    RAMBO supplies foreign affairs information.

APPENDIX II

RELATED READING RESOURCE

1. Balsiger, David W., ed. "Candidates Biblical Score-board." Costa Mesa, CA: *Biblical News Service—Christian Voice,* 1986.
2. Barna, George, and McKay, William Paul. *Vital Signs.* Westchester, IL: Crossway Books, 1984.
3. Brown, Judi. *Prolife Media Handbook.* Stafford, VA: Anastasia Books, 1985.
4. Brown, Judi, and Marshall, Robert G. *School Birth Control New Promise or Old Problem?* Stafford, VA: American Life League, 1986.
5. Chaves, Linda. "Comparable Worth: Issue for the '80s." A Consultation of the U.S. Commission on Civil Rights, Volume 1, June 6-7, 1984.
6. DeMar, Gary. *God and Government.* Atlanta, GA: American Vision Press, 1982.
7. Doner, Colonel V., ed. "The Christian Voice Guide: Strategies for Reclaiming America." Pacific Grove, CA: Renod Productions, 1984.

8. *Final Report of the Attorney General's Commission on Pornography.* Nashville, TN: Rutledge Hill Press, 1986.

9. Gilder, George. *Men and Marriage.* Gretna, LA: Pelican, 1986.

10. Koop, C. Everett. *The Right to Live the Right to Die.* Wheaton, IL: Tyndale House, 1984.

11. Minnery, Tom, ed. *Pornography a Human Tragedy.* Wheaton, IL: Tyndale House, 1986.

12. Nathanson, Bernard. *Aborting America.* Garden City, NY: Doubleday & Company, 1979.

13. O'Neil, June. "The Trend in the Male-Female Wage Gap in the United States." *Journal of Labor Economics,* Volume 3, No. 1, Part 2. Chicago, IL: The University of Chicago, 1985.

14. Peden, Joseph R., and Glahe, Fred R., eds. *The American Family and the State.* San Francisco, CA: Pacific Research Institute for Public Policy, 1986.

15. Saltenberger, Ann. *Every Woman Has a Right to Know the Dangers of Legal Abortion.* Glassboro, NJ: Air-Plus Enterprises, 1983.

16. Schlafly, Phyllis, ed. *Equal Pay for Unequal Work: A Conference on Comparable Worth.* Washington, D.C.: Eagle Forum Education & Legal Defense Fund, 1984.

17. Smith, James P., and Michael P. Ward. *Women's Wages and Work in the Twentieth Century.* Santa Monica, CA: The Rand Corp., 1984.

18. *A Secular Humanist Declaration.* Buffalo, NY: Prometheus Books, 1980.

19. Walton, Rus. *Biblical Principles.* Plymouth, MA: Plymouth Rock Foundation, 1984.

20. Willke, Dr. J.C., and Willke, Mrs. J.C. *Abortion Questions and Answers.* Cincinnati, OH: Hayes, 1985.